MW00635792

CAMPAIGN 406

BORNEO 1945

The Last Major Allied Campaign in the South-West Pacific

ANGUS KONSTAM   ILLUSTRATED BY EDOUARD A. GROULT

OSPREY PUBLISHING
Bloomsbury Publishing Plc
Kemp House, Chawley Park, Cumnor Hill, Oxford OX2 9PH, UK
29 Earlsfort Terrace, Dublin 2, Ireland
1385 Broadway, 5th Floor, New York, NY 10018, USA
E-mail: info@ospreypublishing.com
www.ospreypublishing.com

OSPREY is a trademark of Osprey Publishing Ltd

First published in Great Britain in 2024

© Osprey Publishing Ltd, 2024

All rights reserved. No part of this publication may be reproduced or
transmitted in any form or by any means, electronic or mechanical,
including photocopying, recording, or any information storage or retrieval
system, without prior permission in writing from the publishers.

A catalogue record for this book is available from the British Library.

ISBN: PB 9781472862242; eBook 9781472862211; ePDF 9781472862228;
XML 9781472862235

24 25 26 27 28   10 9 8 7 6 5 4 3 2 1

Maps by Bounford.com
3D BEVs by Paul Kime
Index by Fionbar Lyons
Typeset by PDQ Digital Media Solutions, Bungay, UK
Printed by Repro India Ltd.

Osprey Publishing supports the Woodland Trust, the UK's leading woodland
conservation charity.

To find out more about our authors and books visit
www.ospreypublishing.com. Here you will find extracts, author
interviews, details of forthcoming events and the option to sign up for
our newsletter.

Photographs

Unless otherwise stated, the images in this book are from the
Stratford Archive.

Glossary

ABDA	American–British–Dutch–Australian command
ADRAAFCOM	Advance RAAF Command
AKA	Attack Cargo Ship
ALF	Allied Land Force
DSO	Distinguished Service Order
DUKW	amphibious truck
IED	improvised explosive device
LCA	Landing Craft Assault
LCI (L)	Landing Craft Infantry (Large)
LCT	Landing Craft Tank
LCVP	Landing Craft Vehicle, Personnel
LMG	light machine gun
LSD	Landing Ship Dock
LSI	Landing Ship Infantry
LSM	Landing Ship Mechanized Vehicle
LST	Landing Ship Tank
PT boats	patrol torpedo boat
RAAF	Royal Australian Air Force
SWPA	South West Pacific Area
USAAF	United States Army Air Force

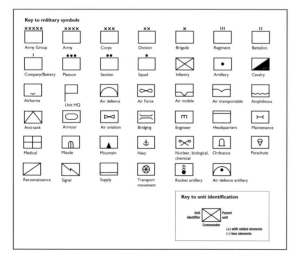

Front cover main illustration: The amphibious landing at
Balikpapan. (Edouard A. Groult)
Title page image: A patrol of the 2/17th Bttn after entering Brunei
town on 13 June.

CONTENTS

INTRODUCTION

Nine days after the attack on Pearl Harbor, Japanese troops landed in Brunei on the South-East Asian island of Borneo. Their primary objective was to secure Borneo's oilfields. Within two months, the entire island had been overrun, and its Dutch and Britain's Indian Army defenders had been vanquished. This, though, was only the start. By early April 1942, the entire East Indies was in Japanese hands. There was some sporadic resistance, but this was summarily dealt with by the Japanese garrison in Borneo. The island remained under Japanese occupation for another three years, as momentous battles were fought elsewhere: in the Solomon Islands, the Central Pacific and in Burma. Effectively, Borneo became a backwater, and apart from its natural resources, it was considered of little strategic importance.

The island lay at a crucial crossroads between the East Indies, Singapore and Malaya, Australia and the Philippines. For the Allies, Borneo lay within Gen Douglas MacArthur's South West Pacific Area (SWPA). As MacArthur's American and Australian forces advanced through New Guinea and the Admiralty Islands, the tide of war drew steadily closer to Borneo. Then, in mid-1944, the naval battles of the Philippine Sea and Leyte Gulf ensured Allied naval supremacy in the region and made large-scale amphibious operations possible.

The main blow, when it came, fell on the Philippines. In October 1944, American troops landed on Leyte and began the reconquest of the Philippines archipelago. At the same time, plans were drawn up for the reconquest of the southern parts of the Philippines and the East Indies, including Borneo. While the Americans would attack the Filipino islands of Mindanao and the Visayas, the Australians would recapture Borneo. The rest of the East Indies were to be bypassed. In theory, Borneo could be too, but political as well as military considerations were at play, and the Australian government was keen to take an active part in the south-west Pacific.

So, MacArthur approved the Australian attack on Borneo. Codenamed Operation *Oboe*, this would involve landings at several points. At 800 miles long and 600 miles across, Borneo is an immense island, most of which was sparsely populated, rugged and clad in jungle. The Allied planners therefore settled on amphibious landings in three key areas: the island of Tarakan in the north-east, Brunei Bay in the north-west and Balikpapan in the south-east. With these in Allied hands, the subjugation of the island would be assured, and all that remained, as MacArthur saw it, was 'mopping up'. After extensive planning, Operation *Oboe* was scheduled to begin in May 1945.

What followed was a surprisingly varied campaign, with Japanese resistance on Tarakan being much more tenacious than the planners had predicted. The Australian conquest of British Borneo was less costly, but it was still a challenging and gruelling operation. The final amphibious attack at Balikpapan in July was also hard-fought, and extensive mopping-up operations followed the capture of the port. The fighting in these widely separated parts of Borneo lasted until mid-August, when the unexpected surrender of Japan brought the fight to an abrupt end. The Borneo campaign was the largest operation undertaken by Australian troops during World War II, and the last. It was certainly costly, claiming the lives of over 2,000 Australian troops, and more than twice that number of Japanese.

While some post-war historians have questioned the value of the recapture of Borneo, for both the island's population and the Allied prisoners freed from Japanese prison camps it represented salvation. With hindsight, the invasion of Borneo could have been avoided, given the imminent end of hostilities in the Pacific, but this was not evident at the time. The success of the Borneo campaign was also a testimony to the professional ability and determination of the Australian troops. Through their efforts and sacrifice, Australia earned a position as an important geopolitical power in South-East Asia. This, then, is the story of what turned out to be the last major Allied campaign in the Pacific War.

Landing craft, in this case LCVPs, pictured during their final approach to Green Beach near Balikpapan on the morning of 1 July. The Australian infantry embarked in them are from the second wave of the 2/14th Bttn. The landing was unopposed, and already bulldozers had been landed to clear away any remaining beach obstacles.

CHRONOLOGY

1941

16 December   Japanese troops land in Sarawak, opening their conquest of Borneo.

1942

January   Australian 7th Inf Div recalled to Australia from Middle East.

11 January   Japanese land on Tarakan and defeat Dutch garrison there.

19 January   British North Borneo surrendered to Japanese.

23 January   Japanese invade New Guinea.

9 March   Surrender of remaining Dutch forces in East Indies.

17 March   Gen MacArthur appointed commander of SWPA.

1 April   Surrender of remaining Allied troops on Borneo.

July   Australian 7th Inf Div committed to New Guinea.

July–November   Japanese offensive in New Guinea halted.

1943

22 January   Buna–Gona region of New Guinea captured by Allies.

29–31 January   Battle of Wau: serious Japanese defeat in New Guinea.

April–September   Salamaua–Lae campaign in New Guinea ends in Allied victory.

1944

February–May   Allied capture of the Admiralty Islands.

19–20 June   American victory in the naval battle of the Philippine Sea.

15 September–4 October   Island of Morotai captured.

October   Morotai developed as Allied base, and headquarters of Australian I Corps.

Australian troops of 2/28th Bttn, 24th Bde, disembarking from an LST on Brown II Beach, Labuan, on 10 May. The relaxed air of the soldiers indicates these men formed part of the battalion's second wave, landing after the beachhead had been secured. The landing was unopposed.

20 October	American landing at Leyte in the Philippines.
23–26 October	American victory in the naval battle of Leyte Gulf.
December	Commencement of bombing raids on oil facilities at Balikpapan.

1945

21 March	Operation *Oboe* approved by MacArthur and planning begins.

Tarakan

11–29 April	Bombing of Tarakan defences by Allied aircraft.
26–29 April	Tarakan Invasion Force sails from Morotai.
27 April	American minesweepers clear approaches to Tarakan.
30 April	Landing on Sadau and clearing of Tarakan beach defences.
1 May	The invasion of Tarakan commences. By nightfall, a beachhead is secured.
2 May	Expansion of bridgehead delayed by Japanese resistance.
3 May	Tarakan town captured, and Australians reach perimeter of airfield.
5 May	Tarakan airfield captured.
6–16 May	Investment of Japanese stronghold of Fukukaku.
12 May	Juata oilfield captured.
17 May–12 June	Continuous heavy fighting around Fukukaku.
13 June	Remnants of Japanese withdraw.
14–25 June	Pursuit and mopping-up operations in north Tarakan.

Brunei, Sarawak and North Borneo

1 June	Brunei Invasion Force sails from Morotai.
7 June	Minesweeping operations commence in Brunei Bay.
10 June	The Australian 9th Inf Div (minus 26th Bde) lands in Brunei and Labuan.
	On both landing beaches, a bridgehead is secured, and Labuan airfield captured.
13 June	Brunei town liberated.
15 June	Limbang captured.

16 June	The first Australians land at Weston in North Borneo.
16–21 June	On Labuan, assault on the Pocket overruns Japanese garrison.
19 June	Landings at Mempakul near Menumbok in North Borneo.
20 June	Landings at Lutong in Sarawak.
21 June	Seria captured, but oilfields set ablaze by retreating Japanese.
26–28 June	Battle of Beaufort: Australian victory secures control of North Borneo.

Balikpapan

10 June	Commencement of air attacks against Japanese defences around Balikpapan.
26 June	Balikpapan Attack Force sails from Morotai.
1 July	Australian 7th Inf Div lands to east of Balikpapan. Beachhead secured.
2 July	Sepinggan airfield and Mount Sepuluh overlooking Balikpapan captured.
3 July	Australians enter Balikpapan.
5–21 July	Rearguard action fought by Japanese around Batuchampar.
5 July	Landing at Panajam on west side of Balikpapan Bay.
21 July	Manggar airfield captured.

6 and 9 August	Dropping of atomic bombs over Hiroshima and Nagasaki.
15 August	Ceasefire: end of hostilities in Pacific Theatre – VJ Day in Britain and Australia.
2 September	Official Japanese surrender in Tokyo Bay: end to the war – VJ Day in US.

ORIGINS OF THE CAMPAIGN

Since 1941, military cooperation between Australia and the United States had reaped substantial rewards. For two years, the two countries had fought together in New Guinea, initially preventing its conquest by the Japanese, and then driving them out of their bases along its eastern coast. The New Guinea campaign was fought in inhospitable terrain and an unhealthy climate. Despite this, and in the face of challenging supply problems, the Allies prevailed. Much of this success was due to the political and military cooperation between Australia and the United States, and a unified military leadership under Gen Douglas MacArthur's SWPA command.

NEW GUINEA

SWPA was formed in April 1942, taking over from the doomed American–British–Dutch–Australian (ABDA) command, after ABDA failed to prevent the Japanese conquest of the East Indies. MacArthur had commanded United States forces in the Philippines, but in February, he was ordered to leave the Philippines and take control of ABDA. When ABDA was dissolved, MacArthur was left in Australia without a job. However, he was the obvious choice to take command of its replacement. As the commander-in-chief of SWPA, MacArthur commanded a theatre of war which encompassed

Australia, New Guinea, the East Indies and the Philippines. He also found himself commanding a mixture of Australian and American troops, as well as air and naval formations. Inevitably, this was a command that required tact, diplomacy and political savvy. However, the often abrasive MacArthur, for all his military abilities, was not known for his diplomatic skill.

One of his first tasks was to form a working relationship with Gen Sir Thomas Blamey, the commander-in-chief of the Australian army. Blamey became the commander of SWPA's land forces, as at this stage of the war Australians made up most of

Australian infantry in the field against the Japanese near Matapau, in Dutch New Guinea, in early 1945. Between 1942 and 1945, the Australian army had fought the Japanese in New Guinea, and had become expert in the kind of fighting that was required of them in Borneo.

MacArthur's land forces. He and MacArthur worked well together, although Australia's Prime Minister John Curtin felt Blamey seemed reluctant to challenge MacArthur when Australian interests were at stake. MacArthur and Blamey faced their first challenge in July, when the Japanese landed in New Guinea. Their advance on Port Moresby raised the spectre of future offensive operations against Australia. Gradually though, reinforcements arrived in Port Moresby, and the Japanese advance was stemmed.

In September, Blamey took personal control of New Guinea Force, and organized the successful joint Australian and American counter-offensive. His first success came at Milne Bay to the south-east of the island in late summer, when a Japanese amphibious landing was repulsed. In the subsequent fighting along the Kokoda Trail between Port Moresby and the Japanese bases at Buna and Gona, the Japanese were driven back towards the island's eastern coast. Then, New Guinea Force spearheaded the US–Australian offensive that by January 1943 had cleared the Japanese from the Buna–Gona area.

The elimination of Japanese resistance at Buna–Gona meant the Allies could move north towards Lae, the largest Japanese base in New Guinea. The previous spring, the Japanese had established themselves in Lae and Salamaua, 22 miles to the south, building airfields and supply bases to support their advance on Port Moresby. In January 1943, fighting erupted at Wau, an Australian outpost inland from Salamaua. The Japanese attack was thwarted by Blamey, who eventually threw the Japanese back. He then ordered an advance on Salamaua from the west by the Australian 7th Inf Div, but this attack stalled in the face of strong Japanese resistance.

However, in September 1943, the Australian 9th Inf Div landed to the east of Lae. This amphibious operation proved a great success. After tough fighting, Lae was captured by the two Australian divisions, and the remnants of the Japanese force withdrew to the north. This meant that by late 1943, southern New Guinea had been liberated.

However, the capture of Lae formed part of MacArthur's fresh offensive, codenamed Operation *Cartwheel*. Its objective was the neutralizing of Rabaul on New Britain, the principal Japanese stronghold in the region. Allied air supremacy in the area, and the consequent control of the Bismarck Sea, played a major part in both the capture of Lae and the success of *Cartwheel*. Essentially, it enabled the Allies to conduct amphibious operations near Salamaua, to support the drive on Lae. After Lae's capture, Allied aircraft were able to neutralize Rabaul, sparing MacArthur the need to subdue it in a costly ground operation. However, Australian and American troops were landed in New Britain that December, and fighting on the island would continue until the end of the war.

Meanwhile, the advance northwards across New Guinea continued. Allied air superiority meant that amphibious landings could be carried out with relative impunity. By mid-1944, the Allies had advanced 400 miles northwards to the coastal villages of Wewak and Aitape. Fighting there would continue until the end of the war. This, though, was largely seen as a mopping-up operation, which would have little impact on the outcome of the war in the Pacific. Effectively, the remaining Japanese in New Guinea were no longer a major threat to the Allies. However, the New Guinea campaign had served as a superb training ground for the Australian army. As a result, its veteran units were battle-hardened, and had gained priceless experience in amphibious operations.

A DIVERGENCE OF INTERESTS

By mid-1944, MacArthur's attention was largely taken up with plans for the reconquest of the Philippines. He answered to the US Joint Chiefs of Staff, and their chosen strategy revolved around two objectives. The first called for SWPA to sever Japan's lines of communication with the Dutch East Indies, the source of most of the oil the country needed to keep fighting. The second was an advance in the Central Pacific so that US forces could secure advance positions for the invasion of the Japanese homeland. In both cases, this revolved around securing air bases that would enable the Allies to establish control of the skies, and so allow the bombing of Japan's remaining territories. That June, the US 5th Fleet's decisive victory over the Imperial Japanese Navy in the Battle of the Philippine Sea ended the threat posed by Japan's carrier strike force – a victory made complete that October in the Battle of Leyte Gulf. As a result, the Allies became undisputed masters of the sea, as well as the sky.

This paved the way for MacArthur's return to the Philippines. The archipelago fitted in perfectly with the Chiefs of Staff's strategic directive, as it sat astride the all-important sea route from oil-rich Sumatra and the oilfields and rubber plantations of Borneo, and the Japanese homeland. Aircraft and naval units based there would be perfectly placed to interdict Japanese supply route and lines of communication.

Effectively, the Dutch East Indies to the south could be left to wither on the vine. Still, in January 1945, before joining its American allies off Okinawa in the Central Pacific, the powerful carrier strike force of the British Pacific Fleet would launch two devastating air attacks on the oil refineries at Palembang in Sumatra, which supplied two-thirds of Japan's oil. These attacks would reduce this supply to a trickle. By then, MacArthur's Sixth Army was firmly established on Luzon and was advancing on Manila, the island's capital.

In theory then, apart from what were essentially mopping-up operations in New Guinea, the Australian army was redundant. The reconquest of the Philippines merely highlighted the dominance of American forces and strategic interests within SWPA. From this point on, Australian land forces would be relegated to a very minor role in the war. Blamey and Prime Minister Curtin were not willing to be sidelined, however. So, several plans were drawn up, designed to give Australian forces a role which had some real strategic relevance.

At the time, British Prime Minister Winston Churchill was keen that the Commonwealth should play a larger part in the closing stages of the Pacific War. He envisaged a recapture of Britain's lost colonies of Malaya, Singapore and Hong Kong. MacArthur, in the meantime, wanted to use Australian troops to relieve American forces tied down in garrison duties.

Blamey took Churchill's scheme to heart and developed plans for a Commonwealth army made up of British, Australian and New Zealand troops, operating as part of MacArthur's SWPA command. In the summer of 1944, though, when he presented this scheme to MacArthur, the American general was horrified. He had no desire to allow the British and its Commonwealth allies to play such a major role in his theatre. So, from that point on, the planning of future operations in MacArthur's SWPA headquarters and in Blamey's Allied Land Force (ALF) headquarters began to follow independent courses.

The Allied landing at Blue Beach on the Gila Peninsula, Morotai, 1 September 1944. This small island in the Dutch East Indies would house the headquarters of Morshead's I Corps, and serve as the assembly and starting point for all three Operation *Oboe* landings.

Essentially, Australia had three options. One was a Commonwealth assault on Singapore from the Indian Ocean, which could then lead to further conquests in the East Indies, Malaya or Hong Kong. The next was a move on Borneo, as a precursor for operations in the South China Sea, such as an assault on French Indochina. The third was closer cooperation with the Americans as they drove northwards through the Central Pacific towards the Japanese homeland. However, Blamey lacked the political backing in Australia to follow such a boldly independent course. Curtin was also unwilling to go against MacArthur's wishes. So, he meekly agreed to the transfer of Australian troops to the Solomon Islands, New Britain and New Guinea, to allow American troops to be used in the planned landing in the Philippines.

Australia had been deftly sidelined, but Blamey and his staff still held a useful card. The command structure of SWPA had been modified, and while the First Australian Army under Lt Gen Sturdee would control operations in these bypassed or garrisoned areas, Lt Gen Morshead's Australian I Corps remained independent of it, although it still formed part of SWPA command. Initially, MacArthur wanted it as his strategic reserve, and planned to use it in a supporting, mopping-up role in his invasion of Luzon. So, Morshead's veteran troops remained in reserve. In fact, when MacArthur's Americans landed in the Philippines, Blamey and the rest of his Australian troops only learned of it over the radio. In November, when MacArthur moved his headquarters to Leyte, the effective segregation of Australian and US forces was virtually complete.

With segregation, however, came a degree of sovereignty. In early 1945, MacArthur announced that SWPA would be divided in two, with the Philippine operation controlled directly by him. The rest would be devolved to the Australians. All Australian headquarters groups within SWPA would be relocated to Morotai Island in the East Indies, in the Moluccas. Morotai had been captured in October 1944, after a month of fighting. Mopping-up operations would continue until the end of the war. MacArthur intended to use the island as a base for American operations against Mindanao in the Philippines.

It and nearby Hollandia in New Guinea were then used as a holding and staging area for the Australian I Corps. However, MacArthur agreed that this formation could be used for a semi-independent operation in the vicinity of the Dutch East Indies. So, with MacArthur's reluctant blessing, the Australians were able to use Morotai as a springboard for their own operation. After considerable thought and planning, the decision was made to use Morshead's troops for Operation *Oboe* – the reconquest of Japanese-occupied Borneo.

BORNEO

Before the Japanese captured Borneo, this vast island was divided into two parts, each ruled by a European power. The southern portion formed part of the Dutch East Indies, while to the north, three much smaller states were collectively under British protection, and so were usually referred to as British Borneo. In 1945, Borneo was divided into four states – Sarawak, Brunei, British North Borneo and Dutch Borneo – the first three grouped on its northern and western coasts. The Raj of Sarawak was the largest of these, which had been claimed by the 'White Rajah' James Brooke in the mid-19th century and was still ruled by his descendant Charles Brooke until the arrival of the Japanese in the capital, Kuching, in February 1942. Although an independent state, Sarawak was a British protectorate.

In its north-east corner was the much smaller state of Brunei. In 1884, the Sultanate became a British protectorate. Although a sultan remained on the throne, the real power was the British resident-general. When oil was discovered there in 1926, the Sultanate became hugely prosperous, and a region of great strategic value. Sure enough, on 16 December 1941, the Japanese arrived in force, and within a week had established control over the tiny realm.

The third state was British North Borneo, another protectorate, which lay to the north-east of Brunei and Sarawak. It had been established in 1876 as a private business venture when the land was ceded by the Sultan of Brunei and the Sultan of the Sulu Islands, but became a British protectorate in 1888. Despite Brunei's oil, North Borneo was the most profitable of the three regions, thanks to farming and the timber industry. This prosperity continued until 16 January 1942, when the Japanese landed at the protectorate's capital of Sandakan. Two weeks earlier, the Japanese Navy had occupied the small semi-autonomous island of Labuan, in Brunei Bay. So, by February 1942, the whole of British Borneo was in Japanese hands.

Tarakan and Labuan were both considered key objectives, as their airfields, once captured, could support further operations in Borneo. Labuan airfield was made operational within days of its capture. Here, a de Havilland Mosquito of 1 Sqn RAAF based at Labuan in August 1945 is being overhauled during operations in support of Australian troops in North Borneo.

An LCI of the US Navy, approaching the landing beach at Labuan, on the morning of 10 May 1945. These large LCI (L) versions were designed to transport a company-sized unit – up to 180 troops – and in theory had a range of up to 4,000 miles. However, conditions on a lengthy passage were uncomfortable.

Dutch Borneo covered the southern two-thirds of the island, although settlement was largely limited to a few coastal enclaves such as Balikpapan on the east coast, Banjarmasin in the south, and Tarakan off the north-east coast. The Dutch East India Company was established in 1602, when it founded the settlement of Batavia (now Jakarta) on Java. Gradually, the company extended its control over the 'spice islands', and in 1800, the territory was transferred to the Dutch government. By the early 20th century, it encompassed neighbouring Sumatra, much of Borneo, the Celebes (or Sulawesi), the Moluccas and the western portion of New Guinea. The discovery of oil boosted the prosperity of this Dutch colony, but the German conquest of the Netherlands in May 1940 cut the Dutch East Indies off from its colonial homeland. On 11 January 1942, when the Japanese invaded Tarakan, the small Dutch garrison there was quickly overwhelmed. The Allies responded by forming ABDA, but even the joint forces of the Allies were unable to prevent the Japanese from sweeping through the East Indies.

In early March, the remnants of the Dutch forces surrendered in Java. Afterwards, the Allies did nothing to recover the region, despite the brutal treatment of the population, the establishment of prisoner of war camps at Kuching and Sandakan, or the Japanese exploitation of the region's oil resources. The Japanese divided the East Indies into three administrative areas, with Borneo being governed by the Japanese 2nd South Fleet, based at Macassar in southern Celebes. Its garrison, though, was supplied by the 37th Army, based in Sandakan (North Borneo). The Dutch East Indies remained a military backwater until mid-1944, when the Allies advancing through New Guinea reached the territory. Gen MacArthur's intention was to recapture all four regions of Borneo, and so deny the Japanese the use of the island's considerable natural resources, and pave the way to further Allied conquests in the East Indies.

The south-west Pacific, 1945

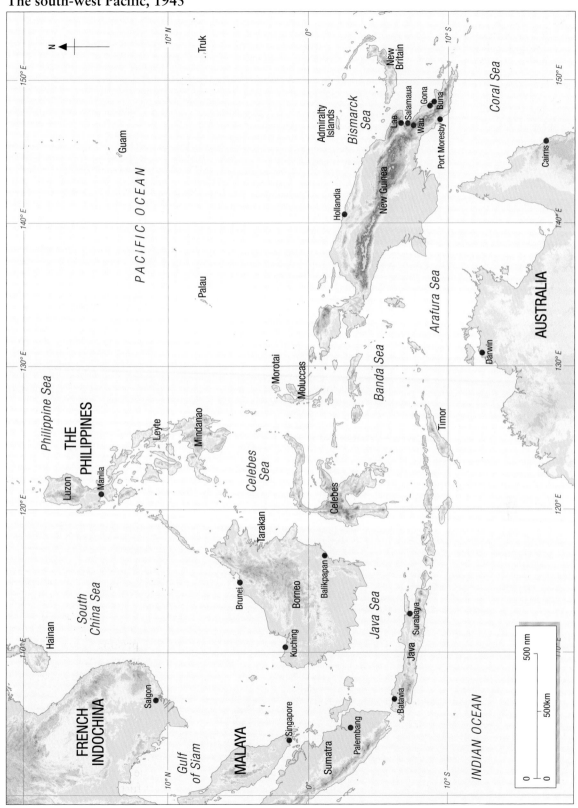

OPPOSING COMMANDERS

ALLIES

The commander of all Allied forces in the South West Pacific Area was **Gen Douglas MacArthur** (1880–1964). Born into an army family, MacArthur attended West Point, before his commission in the US Army's Corps of Engineers. During World War I, Col. MacArthur saw service in France, and in June 1918, he became a brigadier general, commanding the 84th Inf Bde during the Meuse–Argonne offensive. After the war, MacArthur rose steadily through the ranks. He also developed a reputation for being flamboyant, posturing and egotistical, traits which increased after his promotion to major general. In 1930, he became the Army's Chief of Staff, but five years later he was sent to the Philippines to command the Filipino army. Although he officially retired in 1937, while retaining his Filipino command, he was recalled in 1941, and appointed head of US Army forces in the Far East.

Gen Douglas MacArthur (centre), pictured during a visit to Labuan on 10 June 1945. On his right is Lt Gen Leslie Morshead, commander of the Australian I Corps. Explaining the tactical situation to them is Lt Col. Mervyn Jeanes, commander of the 2/43rd Bttn, which at the time was conducting an advance towards Labuan airfield.

When Japan invaded the Philippines on 21 December 1941, MacArthur organized the defence of the archipelago, but was forced to retreat first to the defensible Bataan Peninsula, and then the fortress island of Corregidor. In February, President Franklin Delano Roosevelt ordered MacArthur to escape to Australia before the inevitable surrender of Bataan and Corregidor. In April, MacArthur became the head of SWPA. MacArthur masterminded the campaign in New Guinea and the investment of Rabaul, but he then became increasingly preoccupied with the recapture of the Philippines. Although Operation *Oboe* was approved by MacArthur, there was little direct cooperation between him and his senior Australian commanders.

Head of these was **Gen Sir Thomas Blamey** (1884–1951), who had seen action during World War I at Gallipoli and in France. He left the army in 1925 to become a police commissioner, but he remained in the Australian

Army Reserve. He resigned from the police in 1936 after becoming embroiled in various scandals. However, when World War II began, he became head of Australia's volunteer expeditionary force, and went on to command Australian troops in the Mediterranean before becoming the deputy of the British Middle East Command. After his promotion to general in 1941, Blamey returned to Australia to become Commander-in-Chief of all Australian military forces. That meant he had to work closely with both Gen MacArthur and Australia's prime minister, John Curtin.

Blamey was given command of the predominantly Australian New Guinea Force, and he performed well in the campaign. This, however, came at the price of controversy, with intemperate speeches and clashes with MacArthur overshadowing his military achievements and affinity with his men. More was to come though, as by 1943 Blamey was openly critical of MacArthur's seeming desire to sideline the Australians during the closing stages of the war. Blamey lacked the tact needed to deal effectively with MacArthur. However, the Borneo campaign was largely Blamey's doing, as he saw it as a way for Australia to play a significant part in the shaping of the region after the war.

Gen Sir Thomas Blamey (left), pictured in New Guinea in early 1943, in company with Lt Gen Robert Eichelberger, who was then commander of the US 1st Corps. Blamey had a difficult relationship with his American allies, who he thought were less able than his own Australian troops.

Brig David Whitehead (left), commander of the 26th Bde, pictured on Tarakan on 4 May during the final drive on the airfield there, briefing Lt Gen Leslie Morshead, commanding Australian I Corps. On the right is Lt Col. Douglas, in charge of the 2/11th Field Hospital.

While Blamey commanded Australian troops, the fighting head of these forces was **Lt Gen Leslie Morshead** (1889–1959), commander of the Australian I Corps. During World War I, he served as a private at Gallipoli and distinguished himself there and on the Western Front. He ended the war as a lieutenant colonel, commanding an Australian infantry battalion. After the war, he became a civilian, but he also served in the reserves, and by 1933 had become a brigadier. Like Blamey, he was linked to far-right organizations, but at the outbreak of war this did not prevent his transfer to the regular army. As commander of the 18th Inf Bde, Morshead saw service in the Middle East, where he was given command of a division.

In 1941, Morshead commanded the beleaguered garrison at Tobruk, holding the town for eight months before being relieved. In recognition of his efforts, he was promoted to lieutenant general. By then, Morshead had developed a reputation for success and was noted for resolute and decisive leadership. These skills were demonstrated again at El Alamein in late 1942. In early 1943, he was recalled to Australia and given command of Australian I Corps during the closing stages of the New Guinea campaign. Then, I Corps was earmarked for the invasion of Borneo. With his experience of large-scale operations in North Africa, Morshead was well-suited to the task.

The bulk of Morshead's command was made up of two infantry divisions. **Maj Gen Edward Milford** (1894–1972) commanded the Australian 7th Inf Div, which spearheaded the landing at Balikpapan. Milford was an artilleryman, and during World War I he won distinction on the Western Front, ending the war as a major. He was later appointed the Australian Army's Director of Artillery. In 1940, he commanded the 7th Inf Div's artillery in the Middle East, before being promoted to major general, and sent to New Guinea as commander of the 5th Inf Div. He performed well during the Salamaua–Lae campaign, and afterwards he was given command of the 7th Inf Div when it returned to Australia for rest and refit. In Borneo he proved an able commander, and his understanding of artillery was put to good effect during the *Oboe 2* battle.

The Australian 9th Inf Div, which was assigned the task of the invasion of British Borneo and Tarakan, was commanded by **Maj Gen George Wootten** (1893–1970). During World War I, he saw action at Gallipoli and on the Western Front, where he won a Distinguished Service Order (DSO). Afterwards, he pursued a civilian career, but he remained in the militia. He was also a member of a right-wing paramilitary organization – the 'Old Guard'. At the start of the war, he was recalled to the regular army and was given command of a battalion. He became a brigadier in 1940 and commanded the 18th Inf Bde in North Africa. In 1942, he was sent to New Guinea and took part in the Battle of Milne Bay. Afterwards he was promoted to major general, and given command of the 9th Inf Div, which saw extensive action during the Salamaua–Lae campaign. Wootten was heavily built, weighing over 20 stone, but was surprisingly active, a real 'soldier's soldier'.

Maj Gen Edward Milford, commander of the Australian 7th Inf Div (centre), briefing Gen Blamey (right). On Milford's right is Lt Gen Berryman.

As commander of the Australian 9th Inf Div, Maj Gen George Wootten was responsible for the implementation of *Oboe 6* – the recapture of British Borneo.

Both Wootten and Milford performed well during the campaign and could rely on a handful of experienced brigadiers to carry out their orders. Of these, Brigs Selwyn Porter, David Whitehead and Victor Windeyer of Wootten's division were all called on to conduct largely independent operations, with Whitehead commanding the 26th Bde at Tarakan, Porter the 24th Bde at Labuan and then North Borneo, and Windeyer the 20th Bde in Brunei and Sarawak. Their counterparts from the 7th Inf Div never had a similar opportunity as, during the Balikpapan operation, geography allowed Milford's division to operate as a single coherent command. Even there though, Brigs Frederick Chilton, Ivan Dougherty and Kenneth Eather of the 18th, 21st and 25th Bdes, respectively, all displayed a keen professionalism and empathy with their men. All of these commanders, by this stage of the war, realized that the preservation of the lives of their men was of paramount importance.

JAPANESE

Unlike the Allies, the Japanese had no effective unifying structure of command. Geography dictated this, as not only were the various battlegrounds in Borneo unable to support each other, but any overall command would also be unable to exert much control over the course of the battle. The initiative, after all, rested in the hands of the Allies. So too did complete control of the air and the sea. By this stage of the war then, it was impossible for the Japanese to send reinforcements to areas which were under attack. The Japanese garrisons were very much on their own.

In Borneo, command lay in the hands of the Japanese 37th Army, which was commanded by **Lt Gen Masao Baba** (1892–1947). It was created in September 1944 from the Borneo Defence Army, and Baba assumed command that December. Baba joined the army as a teenager and became a cavalryman, a specialism he retained until elevated to senior command in August 1941, when he was promoted to his final rank. During the inter-war years, Baba had commanded a range of cavalry units, from squadron to brigade, and saw active service in Mongolia during the Sino-Japanese conflict. In December 1941, he assumed command of the 53rd Inf Div, a reserve formation, and the following April, he was given command of the 4th Inf Div, which was based in Sumatra, as part of the 25th Army. Then, in late December, he was sent to Kuching, to assume command of the newly formed 37th Army.

Lt Gen Masao Baba, commander of the Japanese 37th Army, which was based in Borneo. He commanded anti-guerrilla operations there, but he lacked the troops and equipment to offer any real opposition to the Australians during Operation *Oboe*.

In August 1944, V Adm Michiaki Kamada was taken away from naval service with the remnants of the 8th Fleet based in the Solomon Islands and sent to Balikpapan to assume command of the 22nd Naval Special Base Force there. In July 1945, he led the Japanese defence of the port.

While Baba was rightly concerned about the threat of Allied invasion, his primary concern was the waging of anti-guerrilla operations, particularly in Sarawak and North Borneo. During this period, he also assumed the military governorship of North Borneo (now Sabah), and maintained a forward base at Jesselton (now Kota Kinabalu). Although he could do little to counter the Allied invasions when they came, Baba did what he could in the face of challenging circumstances, poor communications and a lack of transport links between the various scattered forces under his command. After the war, he was tried for war crimes and found responsible for the brutal treatment of Allied POWs, particularly during the Sandakan Death March in 1945, and the deaths of over 2,000 Australian prisoners. Baba was hanged in Rabaul in August 1947.

In principle, the 37th Army in Borneo formed part of the Seventh Area Army, which was formed in March 1944 to defend Malaya, Singapore, Borneo and the East Indies from Allied attack. As well as Baba's army, this command included the 16th, 25th and 29th Armies, stationed in Java, Sumatra and Malaya, respectively, as well as a number of semi-independent commands. The Seventh Area Army was commanded by **Lt Gen Seishirō Itagaki** (1885–1948), an experienced field commander who had been involved in the Sino-Japanese War before being recalled to Japan, where he held various staff posts before being sent to Singapore in April 1945 to command the Seventh Area Army. However, he was unable to assist Baba in Borneo during the Borneo campaign. After the war, Itagaki was also found guilty of the mistreatment of POWs and was hanged in Tokyo.

So, with little in the way of support from senior commands, the defence of Borneo was left in the hands of the various commanders on the spot. The most senior of these was **V Adm Michiaki Kamada** (1890–1947). He joined the navy in 1911 and specialized in gunnery. He was given command of a destroyer in 1929 and went on to command the cruiser *Tenyru*. He was appointed to flag rank in October 1941, and served with the 8th Fleet in Rabaul, and saw action in the Solomon Islands and off New Guinea. Then, in 1944, he was sent to Borneo, to assume command of the 22nd Naval Special Base Force, based in Balikpapan. Its primary job was as a garrison to defend the region from Allied attack. So, Kamada commanded both garrison troops and coastal defences, and when attacked in July 1945, he took charge of Japanese forces ranged against the Australian 7th Inf Div. Kamada surrendered to the Allies in September and was eventually tried and executed for war crimes. Elsewhere in Borneo, other regional commanders were left to fend for themselves in the face of the Australian invasion and lacked either the command structure or facilities to organize any form of unified response.

OPPOSING FORCES

ALLIES

During Operation *Oboe*, direct control of all operations lay in the hands of the Australian I Corps, commanded by Lt Gen Morshead, based on Morotai. Under his command were two Australian infantry divisions, the 7th and the 9th. Each had the usual triangular structure, consisting of three brigades, each made up of three infantry battalions, with each of these made up of four infantry companies. Each company had a strength of around 150 men. The brigade was often supported by other units, especially when operating independently of the division. For instance, at Tarakan, the 26th Inf Bde, designated 'Oboe 1 Force' and commanded by Brig David Whitehead, consisted of two additional pioneer battalions, plus additional supporting units.

Whitehead's brigade formed part of Maj Gen Wootten's 9th Inf Div. It was still embroiled in operations on Tarakan when *Oboe* 6 got underway in June 1945. This operation involved the remainder of the division. However, as this involved two separate amphibious landing operations, the division was divided into two brigade groups, each reinforced by one of the division's artillery regiments.

A Bren gun team of the 2/23rd Bttn, pictured on Tarakan on 23 May, during the battalion's attack on the knoll codenamed 'Freda'. Each section of 11 men included a three-man LMG team – a gunner and two loaders.

A 'Frog' in action on 'Tank Plateau' at the northern edge of Balikpapan, during the final clearing of the port by 2/10th Bttn on 3 July. These Frogs were operated by four troops of the 1st Armd Regt, and saw service in all three *Oboe* operations. The flamethrower had a range of up to 90yds.

Both the 7th and 9th Infantry Divisions would normally have been classed as veteran troops, having seen action before in North Africa and in New Guinea. However, both divisions were withdrawn from New Guinea for an extended period of refitting and re-equipping in Australia. During this sojourn, their somewhat depleted ranks were augmented by a sizeable number of reinforcements. In addition, some of the more experienced men in both divisions had been sent to other formations, often after promotion, or had been sent elsewhere after specialist training. As a result, both divisions contained a large proportion of men who had not seen combat before. It has been estimated that these amounted to around 40 per cent of the manpower of these two divisions, and the supporting units which were attached to them for Operation *Oboe*.

A Matilda Mk II tank of the 1st Armd Regt advancing through Balikpapan during the capture of the port on 3 July. Although considered obsolete on European battlefields, its durability and thick armour meant that the Matilda retained its usefulness in the Pacific theatre.

Fortunately for their commanders, enough experienced men remained to guide and train the newcomers. As a result, the combat effectiveness of both divisions was rated as high. In addition, compared to say the US Army, and certainly to their Japanese opponents, the Australians were decidedly more democratic in their approach to military discipline. As a result, leading an Australian formation involved ensuring the men were aware of what was expected of them, and knew why they were fighting. If suitably motivated, then these troops were of exceptional quality, and were more willing to use initiative or to find their own solutions to military problems than other Allied troops in the theatre.

A three-man Bren team, part of a section of the 2/43rd, pictured in action on 13 June, to the north-west of Labuan airfield, during operations to pin and encircle the Japanese garrison. A lance corporal acts as spotter for the gunner, while a loader remains ready to replace the light machine gun's clip.

This said, by the time Operation *Oboe* began, it was clear to everyone involved that the end of the war was in sight. Australia had already suffered a high number of casualties in the war, and the public were keen not to add significantly to this number. So, for both humanitarian reasons and political ones, Gen Blamey and Lt Gen Morshead emphasized the need to keep casualties low wherever possible. To achieve this, the Australian operations in Borneo would be heavily supported by artillery and aircraft, and by naval gunfire. Essentially, the aim was to break the enemy using firepower as much as possible, in order to reduce the Australian body count.

To this end, Operation *Oboe* was heavily supported by both the 13th US Air Force based in the Philippines and from the 1st Tactical Air Force of the Royal Australian Air Force (RAAF) based on Morotai. Both of these formations came under the operational control of Advance RAAF Command (ADRAAFCOM), commanded by AVM Bostock, RAAF. All three campaigns in Borneo were heavily supported by a mixture of Australian and American fighters and bombers. Predominantly, this involved American B-24 Liberators, B-25 Mitchells and P-38 Lightings operating from the Sulu Archipelago, Zamboanga and Samar, and Australian Beaufighters, Kittyhawks, Spitfires and B-24 Liberators flying from Morotai, and later from Labuan. In addition, US Navy fighters and dive bombers were also used, operating from either land bases or aircraft carriers.

Then there was the formidable array of naval and amphibious forces, which together allowed these three large-scale amphibious landings to take place. Even the invasion of Tarakan – the smallest of the three landings – involved the assembly at Morotai of a large armada of 150 ships. At its heart was Task Group 78.1, the Tarakan Attack Group, which was led by R Adm Royal, US Navy, flying his flag in the Amphibious Command Ship USS *Rocky Mount*. His task group was made up of almost 60 landing ships of various types. The two large Australian Landing Ships Infantry (LSI) HMAS *Manoora* and HMAS *Westralia* carried a battalion apiece and sailed in company with the Landing Ship Dock (LSD) USS *Rushmore* and the Attack Cargo Ship (AKA) USS *Titania*. Also in Royal's attack group were 50 smaller landing ships: 22 Tank Landing Ships (LSTs), 12 large Infantry Landing Craft

On Tarakan, after the collapse of organized Japanese resistance, patrols hunted down the remnants of the Japanese garrison. Here, Indonesian soldiers from 2 Coy, 1st Bttn Royal Netherlands East Indies Army (NEI) accompany an Australian detachment from 2/24th Bttn.

(LCI [L]s), 4 Mechanized Vehicle Landing Ships (LSMs) and 12 Tank Landing Craft (LCTs), which were towed by the larger LSTs.

The Naval Attack Force for *Oboe 6* was even larger, and included *Manoora* and *Westralia* again, together with another LSI, *Kinimbla*, and *Titania* and *Rushmore*. Accompanying them were 7 destroyer transports (APDs), 35 LSTs, 55 Infantry Landing Craft (LCIs), 21 LSMs and a dozen or more smaller specialist landing vessels. The largest of the three amphibious operations was *Oboe 2*, which involved a total of 103 landing ships and landing craft, led by the command ship USS *Wasatch*. Once again, *Manoora* and *Westralia* were there, as was *Kinimbla*. In this operation, the Balikpapan Attack Force was supported by a covering force of 27 landing craft armed with guns and rockets, to pour fire into the beaches immediately before the attackers reached the shore.

All of these transports had to be protected. For *Oboe 1*, this involved a protective screen of 12 destroyers, destroyer escorts and frigates, with proportionately more screening vessels for the larger operations. Then there was the covering force, the task of which was to bombard the enemy beaches. For *Oboe 1* and *Oboe 6*, this consisted of three light cruisers and six destroyers, while for *Oboe 2* this included an Australian heavy cruiser (HMAS *Shropshire*), and up to eight light cruisers and 11 destroyers. Most of these were American, but their number also included Australian cruiser *Hobart*, Dutch cruiser *Tromp* and Australian destroyer *Aruntaho*.

In addition, for *Oboe 2* the US Navy provided an escort carrier group for the first few days of the landing, the three escort carriers of which provided dedicated fighter protection for the landing ships and their screen. Other vessels in this armada included fire ships, salvage vessels, survey ships and tugs, as well as PT boats and minesweepers. Few things helped underline the materiel advantage held by the Allies at this stage in the Pacific War than the sheer number and variety of vessels involved in these amphibious landings.

JAPANESE

By contrast, the Japanese troops whose job it was to defend Borneo from invasion were short of supplies and resources, their units were below strength and their troops were not at their peak of efficiency. The Japanese garrison in Borneo formed part of the 37th Army, under the command of Lt Gen Baba. These were scattered around the large island. The 56th Independent Mixed Bde was stationed in North Borneo, while the 71st Independent Mixed Bde was in southern and western Borneo, with its headquarters in Kuching. Another smaller force, part of the 25th Independent Regt stationed in North Borneo, was itself stationed in Labuan. In addition, there were several independent commands, usually of battalion size, scattered around the island, while in both Balikpapan and Tarakan there were naval infantry units, which for the most part were there to man coastal defences. The total strength of these forces was around 31,000 men. This made it comparable in number to the two Australian divisions. The drawback, though, was that while the Japanese were widely scattered, the Australians were able to concentrate overwhelming force wherever they wanted.

In all, there were around 6,800 Japanese troops around Balikpapan, 7,500 in North Borneo, 800 on Labuan, 1,400 on Tarakan, 3,000 in Brunei, 4,000 around Kuching, 2,500 at Martapoera, 3,000 scattered throughout Sarawak, and a handful – up to 2,000 – in posts in the island's interior. Their weakness lay in this need to garrison so much of the island, and in the poor communications between the various points. In Borneo, movement was usually by river or sea, and with the Allies controlling the coast, movement between these various garrisons was severely restricted. Supply problems, too, limited the effectiveness of these Japanese troops, as there was little in the way of stocks of ammunition, or even food, clothing or the other vital necessities of military life.

One factor the Japanese were unable to plan for was the debilitating effect of two things. First, the volume of fire from naval guns and airstrikes poured into the landing areas at Tarakan and Balikpapan for weeks before the amphibious attack sapped the morale of the defenders. This was clear from prisoners who told just how disorienting these relentless attacks had been. Then, after weeks in the field, the physical condition of many of the Japanese soldiers deteriorated, due to a lack of food, unhealthy conditions and almost ceaseless combat. Even the very best Japanese troops would be weakened by this, and many of the men stationed in Borneo were not of the best quality. Still, when cornered they fought hard, and sold their lives dearly.

ORDERS OF BATTLE
AUSTRALIAN

Oboe 1 Force (Tarakan Operation)

26th Inf Bde (Brig Whitehead)
    2/23rd Inf Bttn
    2/24th Inf Bttn
    2/48th Inf Bttn
    2/2nd Pioneer Bttn (engineers)
    2/3rd Pioneer Bttn (engineers, but deployed in an infantry role)

Supporting units
    2/4th Commando Sqn
    C Sqn 2/9th Armd Regt (equipped with Matilda II CS tanks)
    D Coy, 2/2nd Machine Gun Bttn
    2/7th Field Regt (equipped with 25-pdr guns)
    53rd composite AA Regt
    2nd Field Coy (engineers)

Also under Whitehead's command, but not directly part of the brigade structure, was a Dutch infantry detachment and the 2nd Beach Unit.
Whitehead's brigade formed part of Maj Gen Wootten's 9th Inf Div. It was still embroiled in operations on Tarakan when *Oboe 6* got underway in June 1945. This operation involved the remainder of the division.

Oboe 6 Force (Brunei and Labuan Operation)

9th Inf Div (Maj Gen Wootten)
20th Inf Bde (Brig Windeyer)
    2/13th Inf Bttn
    2/15th Inf Bttn
    2/17th Inf Bttn
    2/8th Field Regt (equipped with 25-pdr guns)
    Detachments of 2/9th Armd Regt (equipped with Matilda II tanks), 2/2nd Machine Gun Bttn

24th Inf Bde (Brig Porter)
    2/28th Inf Bttn
    2/43rd Inf Bttn
    2/11th Commando Sqn
    2/12th Field Regt (equipped with 25-pdr guns)
    Detachments of 2/9th Armd Regt (equipped with Matilda II tanks), 2/2nd Machine Gun Bttn

Divisional Reserve
    2/32nd Inf Bttn (drawn from 20th Bde)
    2/5th Field Regt (25pdr guns)
    2/6th Field Regt (25pdr guns)

The 1st Beach Group was divided between the Brunei and Labuan beachheads.

Divisional Units (held in reserve)
    2/7th Commando Regt
    2/12th Commando Sqn
    2/4th Pioneer Bttn (engineers)
    2/3rd composite AA Regt (less one bttn)

Oboe 2 Force (Balikpapan Operation)

7th Inf Div (Maj Gen Milford)

18th Inf Bde (Brig Chilton)
    2/9th Inf Bttn
    2/10th Inf Bttn
    2/12th Inf Bttn

21st Inf Bde (Brig Dougherty)
    2/14th Inf Bttn
    2/16th Inf Bttn
    2/27th Inf Bttn

25th Inf Bde (Brig Eather)
    2/25th Inf Bttn
    2/31st Inf Bttn
    2/33rd Inf Bttn

Divisional Artillery
    2/4th Field Regt (25pdr guns)
    2/5th Field Regt (25pdr guns)
    2/6th Field Regt (25pdr guns)

Divisional Units
    2/7th Commando Regt
    2/1st Pioneer Bttn (engineers)
    2/1st Machine Gun Bttn
    B Coy, 2/1st Guards Regt

Attached Support Units
    1st Armd Regt (equipped with Matilda II tanks)
    Armd Sqn (Specialist Matilda II variants)
    2/2nd Pioneer Bttn (engineers)
    2/1st composite AA Regt
    2/11th Field Coy (engineers)

Also under Milford's command, but not directly part of the divisional structure, was a Dutch infantry detachment and the 2nd Beach Unit, supported by American landing craft and amphibious vehicle detachments.

JAPANESE

56th Independent Mixed Bde
    366th Inf Bttn
    367th Inf Bttn
    368th Inf Bttn
    369th Inf Bttn
    370th Inf Bttn
    371st Inf Bttn

Brigade units consisted of a headquarters based in Brunei, and artillery, engineer and signals formations. These were deployed in Sarawak, Brunei and North Borneo from Miri to Jesselton and Sandakan. The 371st Bttn was based on Labuan.

71st Independent Mixed Bde
    538th Inf Bttn
    539th Inf Bttn
    540th Inf Bttn
    541st Inf Bttn

They too were supported by small artillery, engineer and signals units attached to their brigade headquarters, which was based in Kuching. However, two of its battalions were little more than company-level cadres. One of the full-sized ones was based at Martapoera on Borneo's southern coast, while the other was at Balikpapan.

25th Independent Mixed Regt
This was made up of three infantry battalions. Of these, though, two were transferred to Tawi-Tawi in the Sulu Archipelago. This left only the 2nd Bttn, which was deployed in Brunei, together with anti-tank and engineer detachments.

37th Army
    455th Bttn
    553rd Bttn
    554th Bttn
    774th Bttn

These four independent infantry battalions were stationed at various key points in Borneo. The 455th Bttn was at Balikpapan, the 553rd at Miri on the coast of northern Sarawak, the 554th at Sandakan on the north-eastern coast of North Borneo, and the 774th Bttn was stationed at Tenom, south of Beaufort in North Borneo. While all formed part of the 37th Army, none of them was integrated into the command structure of the two independent mixed brigades. This then, limited their operational effectiveness, rendering them little more than garrison formations. However, by the time the Australians attacked, the 455th Bttn had been moved to Tarakan.

22nd Naval Special Base Force
This unit was stationed at Balikpapan, and was a catch-all formation that incorporated coastal defence gunners, sailors, marines, engineers and airmen. It was formed into two battalions (I and II), based in Balikpapan itself and further inland, at Batuchampar.

2nd Naval Garrison Force
This was also based at Balikpapan. It was made up of armed labourers, base troops and sailors. It also had a battalion-sized detachment at Tarakan, supported by a detachment of around 380 sailors stationed there on the island's small naval base and coastal defences. A similar but smaller formation was based at Brunei, to support Japanese naval operations in Brunei Bay.

Local Garrisons
As well as operational infantry units, several locations in Borneo were garrisoned by static battalions, who manned coastal guns, AA batteries and other defences. They also provided guards for prison camps, and for the protection of key installations. The 40th and 41st Garrison battalions were stationed at Kuching.

OPPOSING PLANS

AUSTRALIAN

The decision to invade Borneo was driven more by politics than military necessity. Until mid-January 1945, Lt Gen Berryman, Blamey's representative on MacArthur's staff, had been sidelined by MacArthur. Then, MacArthur told Berryman that he favoured an Australian invasion of Borneo, despite there being no pressing need for it. As Berryman put it to Blamey in mid-1945: 'The operations in Borneo would have little immediate impact on the war against Japan.' Operation *Oboe* was developed on MacArthur's insistence as a way of contributing to Operation *Montclair*, his strategic plan for the conquest of the East Indies and the Philippines. Apart from *Oboe*, the only part of *Montclair* that was carried out was the extension of American control in the southern Philippines by the invasion of the Visayas islands to the south of Luzon and the capture of the Sulu Archipelago. These operations were collectively known as Operation *Victor* and were carried out by American troops between March and August 1945.

The Dutch East Indies island of Morotai, 650 miles east of Borneo, was the launching point for the Borneo campaign. From October 1944 to June 1945, aircraft based at the island's large airfield complex at Wama were used in bombing missions over Tarakan.

Operation *Oboe*, by contrast, would be an all-Australian affair, save for US naval and air force support, the use of American amphibious vessels and a handful of American beach landing and amphibious vehicle personnel. Once it was completed, MacArthur intended to use Morshead's corps to recapture Java. Planning for *Oboe* went smoothly, largely owing to years of Australian experience in operational planning. It would involve support from the American 7th Fleet, the 5th and 13th Air Forces and the Royal Australian Air Force. At its heart, though, was the Australian I Corps, under the command of Lt Gen Morshead. His force was made up of two Australian infantry divisions, the 7th and 9th, supported by additional units.

Operation *Oboe* – The conquest of Borneo, 1945

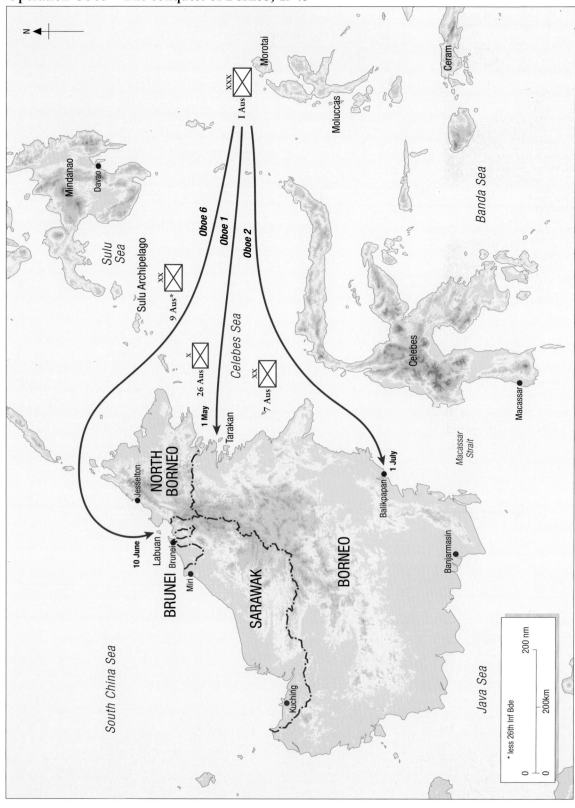

Tarakan airfield, pictured from 'Essex' hill, two weeks after its capture by 2/24th Bttn of 26th Bde on 5 May. It had been heavily damaged, and although airfield construction squadrons of the RAAF worked hard to repair it, it would take several weeks before the airfield was fully operational.

Early on it was decided that the corps would be moved forward to Morotai in the Moluccas, which would serve as the staging point for the operation. The island also housed the headquarters of Morshead's corps. As first envisaged, the operation would consist of six amphibious landings around the coast of Borneo. Of these, however, only three were ever implemented. All would be carried out independently of each other, over the course of several weeks.

Australian infantry of the 2/48th Bttn, watching the progress of the Tarakan Invasion Force on 28 April, a day after leaving Morotai. They were transported to Tarakan in HMAS *Manoora*, a 10,000-ton former liner converted into an LSI, capable of embarking a whole battalion at a time.

A forward observation team, calling in corrections to a heavy mortar bombardment during the advance from the Balikpapan beachhead, 1 July 1945. The Australians possessed a substantial weight of naval, air and artillery assets, and deliberately used them liberally in an effort to reduce the number of friendly casualties.

Oboe 1: The landing at Tarakan Island off the north-eastern coast of Borneo. It would be carried out by the 26th Inf Bde of the 9th Inf Div, with all the relevant supporting naval and air forces. The brigade would be heavily reinforced by additional commando, engineer and armour units, as well as a Dutch contingent.

Oboe 2: An attack on Balikpapan, on the east coast of Dutch Borneo. This would be a full-scale divisional attack, using the 7th Inf Div, and the full range of supporting air and naval assets.

Oboe 3: A brigade or divisional-scale landing at Banjarmasin in the south of Dutch Borneo, to capture the nearby airfields and port. This was to be a follow-on operation to *Oboe 6*, carried out by elements of the 7th Inf Div.

Oboe 4: A full corps-sized amphibious descent on Java, with landings at Surabaya to the east of the island, and possibly also Batavia to the west. This, though, would only take place after the conquest of Borneo had been completed.

Oboe 5: A series of brigade-scale landings at a variety of locations on the Celebes and the Moluccas, designed less to hold territory than to deny regional bases and resources to the enemy.

Oboe 6: A twin landing on the island of Labuan off Brunei Bay, and on Brunei itself. This would be undertaken by the 9th Inf Div, less the 26th Bde, and appropriate additional assets. It would be followed by advances on land through Brunei and Sarawak, and into North Borneo.

In the end, only *Oboe 1*, *Oboe 2* and *Oboe 6* would be carried out.

The first of these, the capture of Tarakan, was scheduled for 1 May. The main objective on Tarakan was the airfield. Once in Allied hands, it could then be used to support operations elsewhere in Borneo. Then, *Oboe 6* would follow in early June. Simultaneous landings on Labuan and Brunei would be followed by further operations in the region, with the aim of securing control of all of Brunei, and the coastal areas of Sarawak. The operation would then be extended to North Borneo. As at Tarakan, the landing on the island of Labuan was primarily to capture the airfields there, which could then be used to support subsequent operations.

Oboe 2 was the largest and potentially most risky of the *Oboe* landings. It would involve a reinforced division landing to the east of Balikpapan, and the port would then be captured in an operation which relied heavily on naval gunfire and air support to achieve its ends. Overwhelming force then was seen as the key to Allied success in Borneo.

JAPANESE

Thanks to the American landings in the Philippines in October 1944, Borneo's lines of communication with Japan had been severed. Similarly, the recent defeats suffered by the Japanese Navy meant it was unable to support convoys in the South China or Celebes seas, which could provide relief for the Borneo garrison. For the garrison, its only effective link with Japan was provided by a few small supply ships, running between Borneo and French Indochina. This meant these garrisons could expect little in the way of reinforcements or supplies. In effect, they were left to their own devices.

The defence of Borneo was entrusted to the Japanese 37th Army, based in Sandakan in the north-east of the island. Although the island could boast a sizeable garrison – the equivalent of three divisions (over 30,000 troops) – these were widely scattered. Most were independent units, which lacked the support provided by divisional assets such as artillery, engineer or tank assets. Also, these were not the highly trained Japanese troops that had first captured Borneo. Rather, they were poorly equipped second-line troops, well suited to garrison and policing duties, but not of the quality expected for front-line operations. Above all, their lack of an effective higher-level command structure would make it hard for Lt Gen Baba and his staff to coordinate their actions. Instead, it was left to individual commanders to respond to the Allied invasion of the island.

The real problem for the Japanese was geography. By necessity, the 37th Army had to defend all the important centres in Borneo, from Jesselton and Sandakan in North Borneo to Banjarmasin on the island's southern coast. The Japanese garrisons were therefore scattered accordingly. This meant that thanks to the almost non-existent transport networks on the island, Baba would be unable to move his troops around in order to react to any Allied threat. Apart from British Borneo, the lack of an effective road network made it hard for the Japanese to respond to any landing by reinforcing the defenders in the area.

To some extent the Japanese made up for this in two ways. First, they had built formidable defences. Experience in the Pacific campaign had shown that defending the beaches was not a viable option, owing to the overwhelming naval firepower available to any attacker. So, the Japanese built defences further inland, constructed from concrete, wood and earth. For example, Tarakan was only lightly defended around the landing beaches, save for an impressive array of mines and underwater obstacles. However, further inland, the Japanese had built a comprehensive defensive network of pillboxes, bunkers, tunnels and trenches. At Tarakan, these defences greatly delayed the Australian conquest of the island.

The general plan was to avoid contesting any landing to avoid the firepower of the warships supporting the amphibious operation. Instead, the Japanese would withdraw to these prepared defences further inland. There they would resist the attackers for as long as they were able. Inevitably though, they would be forced to withdraw in the face of overpowering enemy firepower and numbers. At that point, the Japanese troops would withdraw even further inland and commence what was essentially a guerrilla campaign against the Australian invaders. That would be continued if there were troops and ammunition left to continue the fight.

THE CAMPAIGN

TARAKAN

Operation *Oboe* opened with the invasion of Tarakan. The main objective there was the Japanese airfield. Once captured, Allied aircraft based there could then support subsequent operations across Borneo. The invasion itself was assigned to Brig David Whitehead's 26th Bde, from the Australian 9th Inf Div. Whitehead's three battalions would be augmented by engineers, sappers and commandos, and the whole invasion force supported by a powerful naval task group and by Allied aircraft. The invasion was set for dawn on Tuesday 1 May. Extensive reconnaissance was conducted beforehand through photo reconnaissance flights, covert reconnaissance missions, interviews with former Dutch residents and radio intercepts of Japanese communications. As a result, the planners were able to build a comprehensive impression of the garrison's strength and defences.

The island was 15 miles long and 11 miles across at its widest point. Much of its interior was made up of small steep-sided hills, most under 100ft high, divided by steep-sided gullies. These were covered by a forest pierced by a handful of trails. The exception was the south of the island which encompassed Tarakan town, the nearby airfield, small settlements and the Lingkas oil storage depot. There were also two small oilfields, at Pamusian to

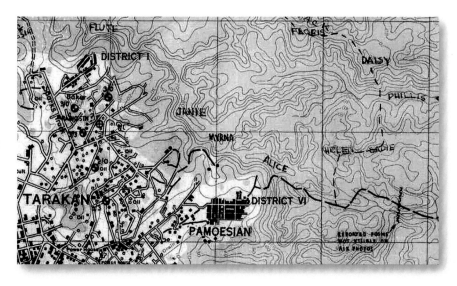

A map showing the codenames for objectives on Tarakan, assigned by Operation *Oboe 1*'s Australian planners. This section, showing the Pamusian oilfield around Tarakan Hill, also included the well-defended 'Helen' feature, along with information about Japanese defences.

the east of Tarakan town and Juata, near the centre of the island. Most of the coastline was fringed by mangrove swamps and was unsuitable for landing operations. The exception was in the south, near Lingkas, where the island's one beach was located. There was no harbour, but jetties and pipelines were used for the shipment of oil or supplies. This muddy beach was the only spot where an amphibious landing might be attempted.

Obviously, the Japanese knew that, and so this beach was well defended. For the Australians, this beach had its advantages, as a tarmac road linked it to the airfield before continuing to the Juata oilfield. Another road connected the beach and Lingkas with Tarakan town and the Pamusian oilfield. The planners dubbed these two roads 'Anzac Highway' and 'Glenelg Highway', respectively. Another important feature was the small island of Sadau, off Tarakan's western coast, where the planners intended to establish an artillery firebase.

P-Day –1

The landing was scheduled for 0845hrs on 1 May (known as P-Day), but two preliminary operations were scheduled for the previous day. Sadau would be captured by 2/4th Commando Sqn, and the 2/7th Field Regt would be established there, where it could support the landings. The beach was divided into three areas – Red on the left, Yellow in the centre and Green on the right. On P-Day, the main landing would be carried out by two battalions: the 2/23rd landing on Green Beach, and 2/48th on Red Beach. Whitehead's third infantry battalion, the 2/24th, would be held in reserve. Before this took place though, a flotilla of American minesweepers began clearing the minefield to the south of the landing beaches. This took three days, but was completed on 30 April, despite the damage to two minesweepers from Japanese fire. Late on 28 April, a flotilla of US Navy PT boats began nightly sweeps off the beach to deter any Japanese attempt to strengthen their beach defences.

At 0740hrs on 30 April, the 2/4th Commando Sqn landed on undefended Sadau Island. By 1100hrs, five 25-pdr howitzers were in place there. It was just as well, as at that moment, the sappers of Maj Foreman's 2/13th Field Coy had arrived to clear eight approach lanes through the underwater obstacles emplaced off the beach. The first of these were 500yds from the shore, rows of iron rails embedded into the seabed. Behind these was a line of wooden posts, while further inshore, more posts were linked together by wire. The clearing operation was due to begin at low tide, to allow the sappers to secure charges to the base of the obstacles. The idea was that Foreman's first wave of 48 sappers would disembark from Alligator LVTs at 1100hrs, screened by smoke dropped from aircraft, and covered by a lengthy naval bombardment of the shoreline, supported by air strikes. Then the guns on Sadau Island would take over the laying of the smoke screen.

Mud-covered and exhausted Australian sappers of the 2/13th Field Coy, recovering after attempting to clear underwater obstacles from the approaches to the invasion beach on Tarakan. This was achieved after considerable effort on 30 April, the day before the main landing.

THE LANDING ON TARAKAN, BORNEO, 1–5 MAY 1945

The campaign began with the landing of the Australian 26th Inf Bde on Tarakan. After preliminary work by sappers, the amphibious assault itself was largely unopposed. This was mainly due to the heavy naval bombardment that preceded it. Once the beachhead was secured, the Australians pressed inland, encountering pockets of Japanese resistance as they went. The primary objective was Tarakan airstrip, but the advance towards it up Anzac Highway was slowed by Japanese strongpoints and extensive minefields. It was 5 May before the airfield was finally taken. Meanwhile, Tarakan town was entered on 3 May, but it took several more days to completely secure it. By then, it had become clear that the bulk of the Japanese garrison had withdrawn to the north. So the battle for Tarakan would continue, amid the dense forests of the island's rugged interior.

16 TARAKAN AIRSTRIP
14

PENINGKIBARU

MANGROVES

ANZAC HIGHWAY

'FI

'RO

RED
YELLOW
GREEN

LANDING BEACHES

2
TAN
HILL
1

BARR

▼ EVENTS

P-Day, Tuesday 1 May

1. 0640hrs: A heavy naval bombardment pounded the beach defences and covered the forming-up of the amphibious assault. It then moves inland as the assault begins.

2. 0800hrs: The first wave of troops land on Red and Green beaches, and quickly secure the beachhead.

3. 0920hrs: The initial objectives of Tank Hill and the former Dutch army barracks are secured. This enables the follow-up waves to land without being overlooked by the Japanese.

4. 1110hrs: On the left, 2/48th Bttn advances up Anzac Highway and secures 'Finch'. On its right, 2/23rd Bttn captures 'Roach' after a brief fight and begins its own cautious advance up Glenelg Highway.

5. 1320hrs: The 2/48th Bttn captures 'Parks' but comes under heavy fire from the vicinity of Collins Highway. This position is eventually taken by nightfall.

6. 1630hrs: 'Pages' is captured, as is the village of Lingkas, but the advance of the 2/23rd is halted at dusk, due to increasing enemy resistance.

P +1, Wednesday 2 May

7. 0740hrs: The 2/24th Bttn resumes the drive north towards the airport and secures 'Sturt' and 'Frank'. The strong Japanese position at 'Wills' is finally taken at noon.

8. 0840hrs: The 2/23rd Bttn captures Lingkas Hill, and by noon, it enters the southern outskirts of Tarakan town and captures the Japanese barracks and defended positions at 'Lyons', 'Jones' and 'Evans', to the west of the town.

9. 1300hrs: The advance up Anzac Highway is resumed, but soon stalls in the face of fire from the Japanese strongpoint at Peningkibaru. The road is so heavily mined and booby-trapped that the advance is halted at dusk.

P +2, Thursday 3 May

10. 0800hrs: The 2/23rd, supported by the 2/3rd Pioneer Bttn, continue to clear Tarakan town and press on to secure the Pamusian oilfield to the east of the city shortly before dusk.

11. 0940hrs: Peningkibaru is captured by the 2/24th Bttn.

12. 1030hrs: The 2/48th Bttn advances through the high ground to the north-east, around 'Butch', 'Sykes' and 'Otway'.

13. 1420hrs: The 2/24th Bttn reaches the south-eastern edge of the airstrip, but further progress is impossible in the face of dogged Japanese resistance. 'Essex' is taken, though, providing a useful observation position.

P +3, Friday 4 May

14. 0700hrs: Fighting resumes around the airfield and continues throughout the day.

15. 1200hrs: Dutch troops attempt to advance to the west of Pamusian but are halted by strong Japanese resistance.

P +4, Saturday 5 May

16. 0940hrs: The airport is finally cleared of the Japanese, but it has been so badly damaged in the fighting that it is far from operational.

17. 1500hrs: Sniping continues in Tarakan, but for the most part, the town is secure. The brigade commander orders a temporary halt to operations, to allow the leading battalions a chance to rest and resupply.

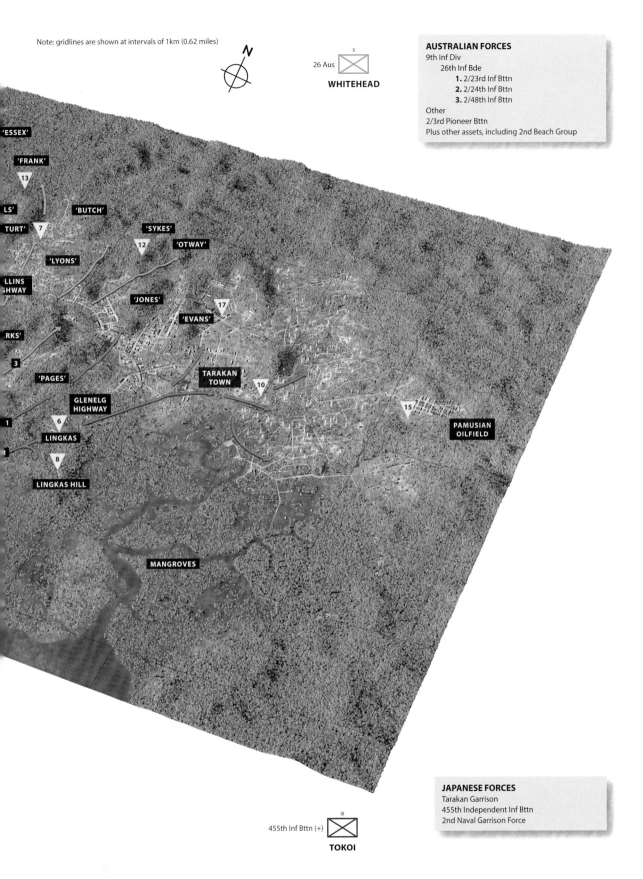

Note: gridlines are shown at intervals of 1km (0.62 miles)

N

26 Aus

WHITEHEAD

AUSTRALIAN FORCES
9th Inf Div
    26th Inf Bde
        1. 2/23rd Inf Bttn
        2. 2/24th Inf Bttn
        3. 2/48th Inf Bttn
Other
2/3rd Pioneer Bttn
Plus other assets, including 2nd Beach Group

'ESSEX'

'FRANK'

13

LS'

'BUTCH'

TURT' 7

'SYKES'

12

'OTWAY'

'LYONS'

LLINS
HWAY

'JONES'

17

'EVANS'

RKS'

3

'PAGES'

TARAKAN
TOWN

10

GLENELG
HIGHWAY

15

1

6

LINGKAS

PAMUSIAN
OILFIELD

8

LINGKAS HILL

MANGROVES

JAPANESE FORCES
Tarakan Garrison
455th Independent Inf Bttn
2nd Naval Garrison Force

455th Inf Bttn (+)

TOKOI

This operation did not go entirely to plan. The smoke-laying aircraft were late, the Alligators went off course, and so it was 1130hrs before the sappers got to work, laying explosive charges while wading through the glutinous mud of the foreshore. Progress was slow, and at 1300hrs, Foreman relieved his first wave with his reserve one, and the work continued, protected by the artillery smokescreen. By 1345hrs, the job was complete, and eight 60ft-wide channels had been cleared. The last of the exhausted sappers were lifted off at 1430hrs. Still, they had been successful, and the way was finally clear for the amphibious attack.

P-Day

The Tarakan Attack Group (TF 78.1) left Morotai on 27 April. This armada of 60 assorted landing vessels included the command ship USS *Rocky Mount*, in which Brig Whitehead was embarked, accompanying the group commander, R Adm Royal, US Navy. His transport group was screened by 12 Allied escorts. The Celebes Sea was glassy calm for the passage, as the transports arrived off Tarakan at 0530hrs on 1 May. Already there was the Cruiser Covering Force commanded by R Adm Berkey, US Navy. He commanded the light cruisers USS *Phoenix*, USS *Boise* and HMAS *Hobart* and six Allied destroyers. Their job was to provide naval gunfire support for the landing and for subsequent operations. Another small transport and escort group carrying the artillerymen, commandos and sappers had already arrived. Also present were the PT boats, the minesweepers and even a survey vessel, there to chart the beach approaches.

Landing operations began at 0630hrs, when the tank-carrying LCTs, which had been towed during the passage, were released, and the smaller infantry- or vehicle-carrying LCVPs (Landing Craft Vehicle, Personnel) were

A heavily overcrowded LST laden with troops and vehicles, crossing the Celebes Sea en route from Morotai to Tarakan, in the days preceding Operation *Oboe 1*. Each of these 4,800-ton vessels could carry over 30 vehicles, 22 Matilda tanks, over 200 troops or a combination of them all.

lowered into the sea, the tracked Alligator amphibians were launched, and the men of the two Australian infantry battalions embarked in their landing craft. Then these landing vessels moved into their assigned positions. Meanwhile, from 0640hrs, the naval bombardment of the shore began, and would continue for two hours. Then, at 0756hrs, landing craft carrying rockets and mortars closed in to join the bombardment, followed by the first of numerous waves of bombers and fighters. One of the watching Australian soldiers recalled that, 'The beach appeared to be an inferno and was continually aflame from the crimson flashes of bursting bombs and shells.'

Under cover of the bombardment, the landing craft were marshalled into positions marked by anchored vessels. Off Green Beach, LVTs were used to transport the 2/23rd Bttn, while off Red Beach the 2/48th was embarked in LCVPs. The reserve force, the 2/24th, embarked in LCVPs and formed up behind the 2/23rd's position. Also, in

The battalion command group of the 2/23rd Bttn, pictured on Tank Hill on Tarakan, shortly after landing there on 1 May. Lt Col. Tucker, the battalion commander, is the third figure from the left, facing away from the camera. His battalion would spearhead the drive on Tarakan town.

the rear were the LCMs carrying the tanks. The landing was scheduled to begin at 0800hrs, at which point the naval bombardment would shift further inland. The Japanese bunkers overlooking the beach had all been silenced. On Red Beach, the 2/48th disembarked from its landing craft without encountering any effective opposition, apart from the knee-deep mud. The beach was quickly secured, and the men pressed on to the Anzac Highway, which led inland towards the airstrip.

On Green Beach, the 2/23rd was having a harder time of it, as its Alligators were stopped by a submerged embankment a few yards from the beach. The men disembarked into waist-high mud, causing some congestion. Still, by 0840hrs, Green Beach was secure, and the leading companies pressed on to take their first objectives, Tank Hill on the left and the old Dutch barracks on the right. Lt Col. Tucker established his battalion headquarters on Tank Hill,

Infantry of A Coy, 2/23rd Bttn advancing over Tank Hill, after securing the feature soon after landing on Green Beach on Tarakan, on 1 May. The empty oil tanks themselves had been badly damaged during bombing raids which preceded the landing.

while his left-hand company joined the right-hand one from the 2/48th, to link up the two beachheads. By then it was 1030hrs. At that point, Whitehead ordered the reserve battalion to land on Red Beach and for the tanks to come ashore. The leading Australian companies were under fire from the high ground near Lingkas, which the planners codenamed 'Roach'. By then, liaison parties in the front line were able to direct naval fire support onto specific enemy targets.

At 1100hrs, the 2/23rd began to advance inland, moving cautiously up the Glenelg Highway towards Tarakan town. On the left, two companies

THE ADVANCE FROM TANK HILL, TARAKAN (PP.38–39)

The Borneo campaign opened with *Oboe 1*, a brigade-sized amphibious landing on Tarakan. This small island off the north-east coast of Borneo was considered of strategic importance because of its airstrip, which the Allies planned to expand into a base for their own aircraft. The landing on 1 May 1945 was preceded by a two-week-long bombing offensive, and then by an intensive naval bombardment as the invasion began. The initial landing was only lightly opposed, as most of the Japanese defenders had withdrawn inland. The 2/23rd Bttn landed on Green Beach, an expanse of oil-slicked mud that proved tough going for the first wave. Eventually, once the beachhead was secured, the battalion was able to press on inland, heading for Tarakan town itself.

This scene shows the start of this advance inland by the 2/23rd during the late morning of 1 May. The Australians are pictured moving north beside the road, which the Australians codenamed the Glenelg Highway (**1**), which led from the beach northwards towards Tarakan town. To the south, behind the advancing Australians, was Tank Hill, a low ridge that overlooked the beach. The oil storage tanks there had just been bombed and shelled, and smoke from oil fires burned there for several days (**2**). At this stage, Japanese resistance was limited to sniper fire, and small pockets of troops hiding in the woods to the right of the road. In this view, one company of the battalion (**3**) spearheads the advance up the Glenelg Highway, supported by Matilda II close-support tanks of the 2/9th Armd Regt (**4**). Divisional engineers led the way, sweeping the ground for the numerous mines and booby traps left there by the defenders (**5**). Overhead, a Bristol Beaufighter of 31 Squadron RAAF (**6**), with its distinctive tiger nose art, is shown flying a ground attack mission, preparing to strafe suspected Japanese positions around Tarakan. The necessarily cautious advance was halted at nightfall, but the town was secured the following day.

moved towards Roach. At 1145hrs, the leading platoon of A Coy came under fire from a pillbox on Roach. This was outflanked and silenced, for the loss of a man. Meanwhile, over to the left, another knoll, Finch, had been taken by the 2/48th, wiping out the Japanese. This meant that the enemy could no longer overlook the beachhead. Lt Col. Ainslie, the battalion commander, established his command post there, as his men pressed on towards the next knoll, Parks, and advanced up the Anzac as it led away from the beach.

The battalion's next objective was a road junction two miles from Red Beach. There, Collins Highway left Anzac Highway and ran east towards Tarakan town. While Parks was taken, enabling the Australians to overlook Collins Highway, the 2/48th then came under heavy fire, and the advance party ground to a halt just short of the road. There were signs that Japanese opposition was strengthening. Still, C Coy, 2/48th crossed the Collins Highway under cover of a mortar barrage, and advanced onto the slopes of the next knoll, Lyons. When darkness fell, the battalion dug in for the night along the highway, and on Lyons, Finch and Parks. It had lost two dead and nine wounded that day, a surprisingly low number, but had made good progress. Meanwhile, Lt Col. Warfe's 2/24th Bttn had landed at Red Beach and had little to do but to brew up tea until the late afternoon, when they were ordered to advance a mile up the Anzac Highway and deploy there for the night. The following morning, they would continue on to the airfield, four miles away to the north.

Meanwhile, the 2/23rd had secured Roach, but the advance up the Glenelg Highway was slow, despite the help of a troop of Matilda II close-support tanks. They took fire from Lingkas Hill, codenamed 'Milko', to the southeast of the road, like an island rising out of the mangroves. To the north, the village of Lingkas had been captured, as had Pages, the knoll above it. Tucker dug in for the night, ready to resume the advance the following day. His battalion had lost just one dead and six wounded. The first tanks had come ashore, but some had bogged down in the mud, as had several landing

A group of LCVPs, with men of the 2/48th Bttn embarked, shortly after disembarking from their large LSI transport, HMAS *Manoora*. These form a second wave and are heading towards Tarakan's Red Beach. Each LCVP could carry a platoon of infantry.

By the afternoon of 1 May, numerous islanders appeared at Red Beach on Tarakan to confirm for themselves that the Allies had come to the island, and their occupation by the Japanese was nearly at an end. Welcome though this was, it helped delay the consolidation of the bridgehead.

craft. Still, American Seabees positioned a pontoon jetty to bypass the mud, while gaps had been cut in the submerged bank off Red Beach. Although the development of the beachhead went more slowly than planned, by nightfall the most serious problems had been overcome, and the Australians were now firmly established ashore.

The Drive Inland

Brig Whitehead's decision not to send the 2/24th towards the airfield was made because he felt it was probable that the Japanese would launch a counter-attack against the bridgehead that evening. In fact, the Japanese decided not to contest the landings, and the expected nocturnal attack never came. So, the following morning the advance was resumed. The priority was to capture the airfield, and so the 2/24th began its advance at 0730hrs, supported by tanks, artillery fire and air strikes. On the right, the knoll Sturt was captured by 0900hrs, and by noon, the battalion's leading company had secured Frank, 1,000yds to the north. However, on the left, progress was much slower. The knoll Wills was protected by a network of trenches, pillboxes and machine-gun bunkers. An attempt to outflank these defences from Sturt was thwarted by a minefield.

By noon, the position was taken after an airstrike by US Mitchell bombers, heavy artillery bombardment and an attack using flamethrowers. The advance towards the airfield could be resumed. Fighting continued though, with Wills taken for the loss of two Australians and 19 Japanese. While on the right of the road, the forest-clad knoll Essex, a mile to the north, was designated as the next objective. However, the leading companies soon came under fire from Japanese naval infantry entrenched in the village of Peningkibaru. It proved hard to oust them, as the approach to the village was mined. Later, the Australians claimed they had encountered more mines on Tarakan than they had anywhere else in the Pacific. While most were conventional, others were improvised explosive devices (IEDs).

A troop of Matilda tanks fired into the village, but they were pulled back after one Matilda detonated a 250kg bomb buried beside the road. Amazingly, only one of its crew was injured. Engineers were called up, and progress was slow as they probed their way forward, uncovering mines and IEDs as they went. When the supporting infantry came under fire, they jumped into the roadside ditches, only to discover they too were seeded with explosives. Meanwhile, Peningkibaru was pounded by artillery and aircraft. In the end, it was found that progress was only possible by wading through the swampy ground to the left of the road. Dusk fell shortly after 1830hrs, by which time the leading Australian units were still short of Essex, and had not captured Peningkibaru. That evening, the airfield, 1,000yds beyond the Japanese-held village, seemed a long way away.

Meanwhile, on Wednesday, the advance on Tarakan town had also resumed. Lingkas Hill was taken without opposition, the Japanese there having withdrawn, but a little further on, the 2/23rd came upon a complex of pillboxes, trenches and tunnels. This held up the advance for the rest of the day, as the position was pounded by artillery. However, the following morning revealed the Japanese had withdrawn. On Thursday morning, the advance continued, and the Australians finally entered the town. Back on the beachhead, the build-up continued. The pontoon jetties greatly eased the whole business of landing vehicles, men and supplies. The problems continued ashore though, as the congested beachhead became a confused mass of vehicles, stores and reinforcements. The situation eased a little by Wednesday afternoon, as the expansion of the bridgehead enabled the rear echelons to expand along the Anzac and Glenelg Highways.

The substantial nature of the Japanese defences on Tarakan came as a surprise to the Australians. Here, a wood, earth and concrete pillbox on Essex is cleared by the 2/24th Bttn on 5 May after an extensive naval bombardment.

On the morning of Thursday 3 May, the 2/23rd entered Tarakan, where locals told them the Japanese had pulled out. It was the same in District IV, where the Japanese had left behind a network of tunnels and bunkers. Sniping, though, remained a problem as the Australians pushed on through Tarakan. This opposition increased as they approached the Pamusian oilfield complex on Tarakan Hill. The Australian advance was duly halted as the position was bombarded by artillery and naval guns. Fighting continued around the ridge near the hospital, on the eastern side of Tarakan town. The Japanese there were a rear guard charged with buying time for the rest of the Japanese garrison to pull back into the island's interior. Initial attacks by the 2/23rd were repulsed, and some Japanese groups even counter-charged their assailants with bayonets.

That night, 3/4 May, Whitehead withdrew the 2/23rd, replacing it with the fresh 2/3rd Pioneer Bttn, which was better equipped to deal with booby traps and static defences. It was supported by the 2/4th Commando Sqn. On Friday morning, the commandos fought their way up Tarakan Hill, supported by Matilda tanks, and cleared the network of defensive works to reach the crest by 1215hrs. However, two concrete pillboxes remained, and it took the rest of the day to silence them. Although the Japanese ceded the oilfield to the Australians, a group of defenders remained trapped in the hill's network of tunnels. The Pioneers simply sealed their entrances with explosives, leaving the Japanese soldiers entombed inside. By Saturday morning, the Pioneers had cleared Tarakan town, and established positions around the town, from Lyons and Otway in the west to Pamusian and District IV to the east.

Meanwhile, on Anzac Highway, the advance resumed on Thursday morning. The 2/24th launched a determined assault on Essex, supported by tanks, and the knoll was captured by mid-afternoon. The attackers, though, faced a series of spirited Japanese counter-attacks before they could be reinforced. A dawn attack by the 2/24th on Peningkibaru cleared the troublesome village by 1200hrs, as the surviving defenders withdrew to the north. That left the way clear for a final drive onto the airfield. At 1638hrs, the 2/24th began a set-piece attack across the main runway towards 'Rippon', a low knoll on the north side of the airfield. Its Japanese defenders could easily cover the whole airfield, so the place was the key to its defence. The assault was covered by smoke and supported by artillery. While enemy fire was heavy, booby traps were a bigger problem, and two huge mines were detonated, which virtually wiped out the leading platoon. Still, the attackers finally reached the ruins of the airport buildings, and so established a toehold on the airfield. Rippon, however, remained just out of reach.

On the night of 3/4 May, there was continued fighting, as small groups of Japanese launched counter-attacks. Late on Friday morning, another attack on Rippon was launched, but it seemed that most of the defenders had withdrawn during the night. This key knoll was captured by 1530hrs. This effectively meant that Tarakan airfield was in Australian hands. As a flag was raised over its bomb-shattered runway and ruined buildings, and the 2/24th Bttn consolidated its hold on the airfield, Brig Whitehead finally realized exactly what his men were facing. They had been fighting a tenacious rear guard. The bulk of the Japanese garrison had withdrawn into the island's rugged interior. That meant that securing the airfield was only part of the battle for Tarakan. The much harder fight still lay ahead.

The Battle for Tarakan, May–June 1945

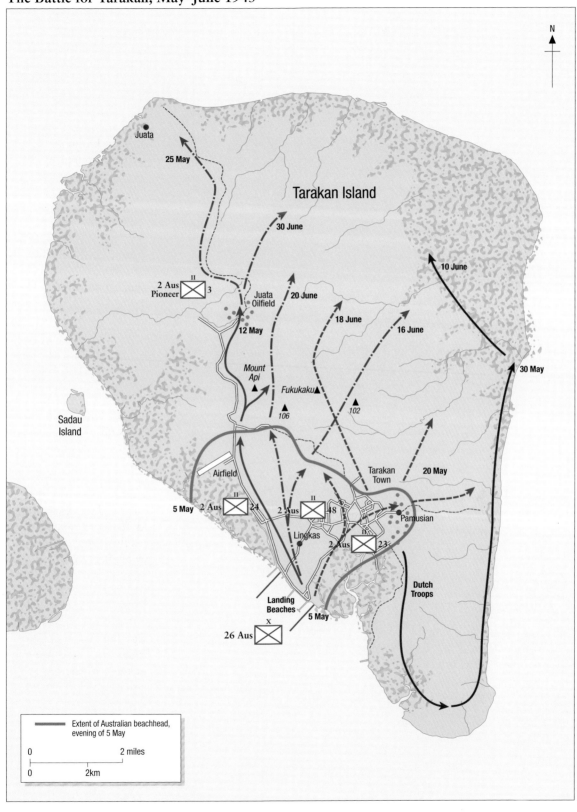

Juata

25 May

Tarakan Island

2 Aus
Pioneer [II / 3]

30 June

10 June

Juata
Oilfield

20 June

18 June

16 June

12 May

30 May

*Mount
Api* ▲

Fukukaku ▲

106

▲
102

Sadau
Island

Tarakan
Town

20 May

Airfield

5 May 2 Aus [II / 24] 2 Aus [II / 48]

Pamusian

Lingkas

2 Aus [II / 23]

Dutch
Troops

Landing
Beaches

5 May

26 Aus [X]

Extent of Australian beachhead,
evening of 5 May

0   2 miles

0   2km

The Fight for the Interior

In the battle that followed, the fighting would be fought by infantry. While artillery could offer support, identifying targets was hard in this terrain. The Japanese were also able to make good use of their prepared positions. What followed would be the hard-fought climax of the Tarakan campaign. As MacArthur later put it:

> Fierce hand-to-hand fighting broke out along the ridges and in the jungle. Fanatic suicide charges were made by the Japanese defenders as they counter-attacked with savage determination. The Japanese were driven into the hills east of the airfield, where they fell back to well-prepared ground, to continue a dogged resistance. Tanks blasted the Japanese from their holes and trenches, while repeated infantry attacks reduced their defences to small individual pockets.

This understated account hides much of the brutality of this short, intense engagement.

After securing the airfield, the 2/23rd pressed on up the Juata road towards Mount Api ('The Mountain of Fire' in the Dyak tongue). There the battalion met fierce resistance on 'Tiger', Api's south-eastern spur. Some 200 Japanese defenders held a strong position there, protected by yet more pillboxes and trenches. On 7 May, the battalion gained a foothold on this spur, only to be forced back by a spirited Japanese counter-attack. The following day, the Australians tried again, and this time managed to regain the ground, before working their way up Tiger. Unfortunately, the Japanese defenders proved hard to budge, despite heavy air and artillery attacks.

However, Tiger was only a prelude. The real centre of the Japanese defence was known as 'Fukukaku'. This was not really a single hill at all – it was more an interlocking series of steep-sided ridges, spurs and knolls, all covered by thick forest and dense undergrowth. This made it a defender's dream. Fukukaku was also covered in pillboxes, bunkers, trenches and minefields. The Japanese field headquarters was there, as was its main field hospital and several small guns. This formidable position was occupied by marines of the 2nd Naval Garrison, and the regular infantry of Tokoi Force, all under the direct command of Maj Tadai Tokoi. This fight for Fukukaku would be the real climax of the battle.

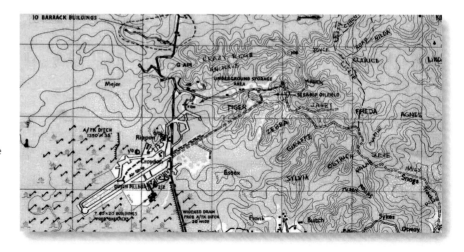

Another detail from the map drawn up by Operation *Oboe 1*'s planners, focusing on the codenamed features around Tarakan airfield, and the Fukukaku area, centred around Hill 105, and the ridges, spurs and knolls codenamed 'Joyce', 'Margy', 'Clarice' and 'Freda'. Each map square is scaled at 1,000yds.

Fukukaku was linked to the Australians on Mount Api by Crazy Horse Ridge. This narrow spine of high ground ran eastwards for a mile from Mount Api to Hill 105, the first of the outlying complex of hills and ridges that made up Fukukaku. It lay half a mile north of Tiger, the spur of which joined the larger ridge just below Hill 105. This was the obvious line of approach for Whitehead. It was there, on 8 May, that word reached the 2/23rd Bttn that Germany had surrendered. Many of the men had fought against the Germans in North Africa, but on Tarakan they did not have time to celebrate. They were locked in battle with another enemy. Still, the extra issue of beer was welcomed by the exhausted soldiers.

Brig Whitehead's intention was to pin the Japanese defenders on Fukukaku and cut off their line of retreat. Then he planned to use air strikes and artillery barrages to support company-level attacks by his four battalions, nibbling away at the defences, to constrict the Japanese. First though, he had to reach the place. On 9 May, the exhausted 2/23rd Bttn was relieved by the 2/24th. It would clear Tiger, and advance eastwards along Crazy Horse Ridge to pin the Japanese defenders on Hill 105.

The 2/24th began its attack on 9 May, in the face of strong Japanese opposition. A simultaneous attack was launched against Tiger. The razor-backed summit of the ridge meant that no more than a platoon could attack at any one time, supported by Matilda tanks, flamethrowers and artillery. The Japanese fought stubbornly, and progress was excruciatingly slow. It was worse at night, as Japanese platoons tried to infiltrate the Australian lines, resulting in sudden assaults and tensely fought firefights at point-blank range. However, each morning the advance continued, and by 11 May, the battalion had reached the western slopes of Hill 105.

This proved to be a particularly strong position, protected by pillboxes and machine-gun bunkers. The battalion halted for a day to rest, while artillery and airstrikes pounded the hill, and P-38 Lightnings dropped napalm on its summit. This had the advantage of clearing the cover on the summit, making the Japanese positions more visible. The lower slopes, however, were covered in felled trees and branches, which were hard to penetrate, especially in the face of Japanese fire. Whitehead ordered the 2/24th to resume the attack on 13 May, but this time to bypass Hill 105, and instead to assault 'Joyce', the spur to the east of it that linked the hill to the rest of the Fukukaku position. With it in Australian hands, the defenders of Hill 105 would be completely isolated.

After being heavily bombed, shelled and napalmed, Hill 105 on Tarakan was largely stripped of cover. However, its lower slopes became a tangle of felled trees and uprooted vegetation, which made progress difficult for the Australians. This photograph was taken on 29 May, ten days after the hill was captured by the 2/24th Bttn.

Meanwhile, the 2/24th also managed to send a company up the road leading north from the airfield, supported by a troop of tanks. Opposition here proved light, and the Juata oilfield was reached on 9 May. However, it took another three days to clear the surrounding area of any remaining defenders. Another company finally managed to clear the summit of Tiger, which meant the airfield was no longer under observation from the Japanese.

A Matilda close-support tank of C Sqn, 2/9th Armd Regt on Tarakan, during the attack on Sykes, a knoll to the west of Tarakan town on 6 May. The tank is supported by soldiers of C Coy, 2/48th Bttn.

Simultaneously, the 2/4th Commando Sqn was ordered to advance from Tarakan town along Snag's Track, which wound its way north-westwards, beneath Fukukaku to reach the metalled Juata road near Mount Api. This was important, as it helped consolidate the Australian front line and enabled the Matildas to support the main attack. By 12 May, the commandos reached 'Susie', a mile to the south-east of Fukukaku. Following the commandos were the Pioneers, who improved the track so jeeps could bring up supplies, and casualties could be evacuated along it. Similar work was being carried out on all roads and tracks leading to the front line.

This highlighted one of the strange features of the Tarakan battle. A soldier could be shot on one side of a ridge, while on the other, less than a mile away, was a casualty clearing station, while a mile behind that was a fully functioning field hospital, positioned close to dug-in artillery batteries, supply dumps and rest areas. Secure font lines did not exist on Tarakan, and the Japanese launched several night-time sorties against the Australian rear areas including the field hospital. Some of the Japanese raiders even carried spears so they could attack without the noise of gunfire alerting the defenders. Others laid IEDs and booby traps to sow confusion in the Australian rear. Ultimately, none of these sorties achieved much, apart from increasing tension.

During a visit by Gen Blamey to Tarakan on 8 May, Whitehead reiterated that he intended to use firepower and support to keep Australian casualties to a minimum. He explained that his brigade was pinning Fukukaku, with the 2/24th

Snag's Track on Tarakan ran north-west from Tarakan town, and joined the main Juata road beside Mount Api. This bend in it lay between Tiger and Crazy Ridge, a mile east of the Mount Api junction, and reveals the challenging terrain the Australians faced there.

to the north-west, the 2/23rd to the south-west and the 2/48th to the east. Once the enemy was pinned in place, Whitehead intended to encircle the Japanese position. This process began on 13 May with the attack by the 2/24th on Joyce. It attacked from the west, bypassing Hill 105 to the north, while the 2/48th would advance on Joyce from the east, by way of another summit, Hill 102.

Here the high ground was more rounded, forming a series of linked knolls, which ended in the west with Joyce. With this done, and Joyce in Australian hands, the encirclement of Fukukaku would be complete. In the east, the advance of the 2/48th was surprisingly rapid, as this area was largely devoid of Japanese troops. Hill 102 was captured, but opposition increased around the knoll codenamed 'Hilda', 400yds east of Joyce. Still, it meant that the Australians were gradually closing in on the Fukukaku position, and the net around it was drawing tighter.

Meanwhile, the 2/3rd Pioneers and a company of Dutch infantry were still on Tarakan Hill and faced the task of clearing the Japanese from the south-eastern side of the island. On 7 May, they began their advance, which was quickly stalled by strong Japanese resistance centred on a hilltop codenamed 'Helen', a mile to the east of Pamusian. The hill was covered in tunnels and machine-gun bunkers, defended by two companies of Japanese infantry led by Lt Hiroichi Fudaki. A set-piece attack on it was called off, and instead, on 10 and 11 May, Helen was pounded by artillery and bombed by American Liberator bombers. Napalm was also dropped by P-38 Lightnings.

On 12 May, the attack on Helen was resumed, and Cpl John Mackey was awarded a posthumous Victoria Cross after capturing three machine-gun bunkers on the hill's crest. The Japanese still hung on though, the remnants only withdrawing on 14 May. They left behind numerous booby traps, which the Pioneers spent the next two days clearing. Meanwhile, the Dutch company advanced along the track leading to Cape Batu, the southernmost tip of Tarakan, encountering very little resistance. There, a detachment of the Dutch company used LCMs to probe the mangrove swamps and inlets on the south-east side of the island, working its way north to link up with the Pioneers and the rest of the company near the coast, directly east of Pamusian. So, on 16 May, with this part of the island secure, the Pioneers moved north, to support the rest of the brigade.

While this was all playing out, the battle for Fukukaku continued. For four days from 14 May onwards, the Australians probed the Fukukaku defences, to see exactly where they lay. Its western side was anchored on Hill 105, then ran south to encompass the spurs 'Margy' and 'Janet' before it crossed Snag's Track to the knolls 'Ostrich' and 'Susie'. On 15 May, the commandos seized the unoccupied 'Agnes', on the defence's eastern side, and held it in the face of two counter-attacks. Then, on 18 May, the 2/24th attacked Hill 105, and eventually gained a foothold on its bomb-cratered summit. The following day, the 2/48th attacked the line of knolls overlooking Snag's Track, with mixed results. Some ground was taken, but the knoll 'Freda', 400yds west of Agnes, remained in Japanese hands. Freda was then pounded by bombs and napalm for three days, before another assault was launched by the 2/48th on 22 May, attacking from Agnes. The Japanese held on though, and the Australians withdrew after suffering heavy casualties. So, apart from Hill 105 and the small knolls directly beside Snag's Track, the Japanese perimeter was holding.

On 24 May, the commandos discovered that Susie, a knoll just to the south of Freda, had been abandoned. It seemed that the Japanese were pulling back and consolidating their perimeter, with Freda, Margy and Clarice forming its inner defence, a position covering approximately a square mile. That afternoon the Australians gained a foothold on Margy, helped by artillery that had deployed south of Snag's Track and fired directly at the summit. Somehow, though, the Japanese defenders held on. As Whitehead's guns were short of ammunition, he decided to limit their use to supporting one attack per day. He began with the 2/24th, which after securing Hill 105 had extended its encirclement of Fukukaku by attacking the knolls 'Beech' and 'Poker', a mile to the north. This would allow the use of the 'Dutch track' from Juata oilfield to bring up supplies directly to the battalion's perimeter. The knolls were bombed for several days, and on 1 June the Australians launched an attack, only to find that the defenders had withdrawn during the night.

Meanwhile, on 31 May, the bombers pounded Margy, where the 2/23rd finally managed to gain the summit. It took another day to clear the network of tunnels dug into the hilltop. There was a pause in the fighting as supplies were brought up, while the bombers and artillery pounded the reduced Japanese perimeter. Meanwhile, the Australians strengthened their own grip around Fukukaku by taking two more knolls to the north, allowing the 2/24th and 2/48th to link up a mile north of the Japanese position. Then, during the night of 10/11 June, there was activity within the Japanese perimeter, and Japanese attacks were launched against the boundary of these two Australian battalions. In the morning, the Australians discovered the Japanese perimeter had shrunk again, and was concentrated on Joyce, 500yds east of Hill 105, and 600yds north of Margy – the very heart of the Fukukaku position. Joyce became the fresh target for Allied bombers and napalm-armed fighters. Then, on the morning of 14 June, patrols discovered the hilltop had been abandoned during the night. Somehow, the Japanese had slipped through the Australian lines and escaped. The Battle of Fukukaku was over.

By 10 June, when this photograph was taken, the knoll codenamed 'Margy' was turned into an improvised Australian firebase called HMAS Margy. Its guns – a mixture of 25-pdrs and AA guns – were used to fire directly at the Japanese on nearby 'Joyce' ridge, just 500yds away.

After the withdrawal of the Japanese from their Fukukaku stronghold, the Australians pursued them towards the north. Here, on 21 June, a patrol of the 2/24th Bttn advances up the shallow Selajong River in northern Tarakan, searching for remnants of the Japanese garrison.

In fact, Tokoi had been thinning his lines for several days, slipping men out through the Australian lines to the east. At 0400hrs on 14 June, the final troops left, and the wounded left behind committed suicide. Intelligence suggested that the Japanese had about 800 soldiers left and were desperately short of food and ammunition. While mopping up continued on Fukukaku, the bulk of the Australian brigade set off in pursuit. That evening the Japanese rear guard repulsed an Australian probe, but this was only a brief setback, and the pursuit gathered pace. Landing craft moved detachments of troops up Tarakan's eastern coast, while the PT boats patrolled the northern shore of the island. On 20 June, some 200 Japanese made another brief stand on Hill 90, three miles east of the Juata oilfields, but this defence dissolved in the face of sustained mortar attacks. This was the last of any organized resistance on Tarakan.

By 24 June, it was clear that all that was left was a mopping-up operation. Brig Whitehead therefore divided the island into four areas. Each battalion was responsible for its own area, and for clearing any remaining Japanese from its perimeter. Air and naval sweeps over the sea to the north resulted in a string of prisoners, captured on homemade rafts as they tried to flee to the mainland. On Tarakan, 200 more Japanese were captured during the following weeks. The real fighting, though, was over. Tarakan was now firmly in Australian hands.

The reason the island had been attacked was to secure its airfield. However, the airfield would take several weeks to repair, as the waterlogged ground made it hard to extend it without major work. It would take two months before it was fully operational, and by then the war was virtually over. Instead, air support for the operations around Brunei, North Borneo and Balikpapan came from the airfield on Tawi-Tawi in the Sulu Archipelago, 180 miles to the north of Tarakan, or from Allied aircraft carriers. The invasion of Tarakan had cost the Australians almost 900 casualties: 225 killed and 669 wounded. The Japanese toll was even higher: 1,540 killed and 252 captured. The capture of the airfield was not worth the lives of so many men. Afterwards, an RAAF report stated of its seizure: 'Had the correct information been available, it is doubtful whether the project would have been attempted.'

BRITISH BORNEO

Five weeks after the start of *Oboe 1*, the Australians unleashed *Oboe 6* – the invasion of British Borneo. The main objective of *Oboe 6* was the capture of Brunei Bay. As the divisional orders put it, the objective was to 'secure the Brunei Bay area of North Borneo, to permit establishment of an advanced naval base, and to protect oil and rubber resources therein'. To achieve this, Lt Gen Morshead allocated Maj Gen Wootten's 9th Inf Div for the task, less the 26th Inf Bde, which was still on Tarakan. This would have additional supporting units, as well as a sizeable naval force and extensive air assets. *Oboe 6* was a complex operation, and the largest amphibious assault yet attempted by the Australians.

Brunei

The assault force left Morotai on 4 June, and arrived in Brunei Bay at dawn on Sunday 10 June. While the 24th Inf Bde would assault the island of Labuan, Brig Windeyer's 20th Inf Bde would recapture Brunei and Sarawak. He had three experienced infantry battalions under his command, the 2/13th, the 2/15th and the 2/17th. Two would lead the assault, while the 2/13th was held in reserve. The infantry were supported by the 25-pdrs of the 2/8th Field Regt, the 1st Beach Group and detachments from the 2/9th Armd Regt, the 2/2nd Machine Gun Bttn and 9th Div's engineers.

Each battalion had its own landing area. The 2/17th would assault Green Beach, to the north-east of Brooketon (now incorporated into Muara), which lay at the end of a small peninsula a few miles north of Brunei itself. The 2/15th would make a simultaneous landing on White Beach, which was on the north-east side of marshy Muara Island, which overlooked the south-east approach to Brooketon. A third and more sheltered landing area, Yellow Beach (now Muara Port), was where Windeyer planned to land tanks and supplies. Intelligence reports suggested that Muara Island had a Japanese garrison, and so this had to be neutralized before Yellow Beach could become operational. This also depended on the 2/17th securing this third landing area. Without it, Green Beach alone was too exposed to use as a landing area for the brigade's heavy equipment and vehicles. Then, the brigade would press south from Brooketon towards Brunei town (now Bandar Seri Begawan).

The operation began at 0815hrs on 10 June. A naval bombardment pounded White and Green beaches, as LSI *Kanimbla*, carrying the bulk of the 2/17th Bttn, approached Green Beach. The troops transferred into smaller landing craft for the beach assault. At 0906hrs, these began their approach, supported by rocket-firing landing craft. The first wave reached the beach at 0918hrs, and quickly discovered there were no Japanese there to oppose them. By noon, both Brooketon and Yellow Beach had been captured, and the bridgehead secured.

Meanwhile, the first wave of the 2/15th stepped ashore on White Beach at 0915hrs. It was soon discovered that the swampy Muara Island was undefended; the rest of the brigade could begin landing on Yellow Beach. In fact, the only Japanese encountered that day was a five-man patrol, which was ambushed outside Brooketon. Windeyer landed his reserve battalion, and by sunset, his perimeter extended two miles inland. The night was quiet, apart from one minor clash with a Japanese patrol, and a prisoner told his Australian captors that they had no idea the enemy had come ashore.

The invasion of Brunei and Sarawak, June–July 1945

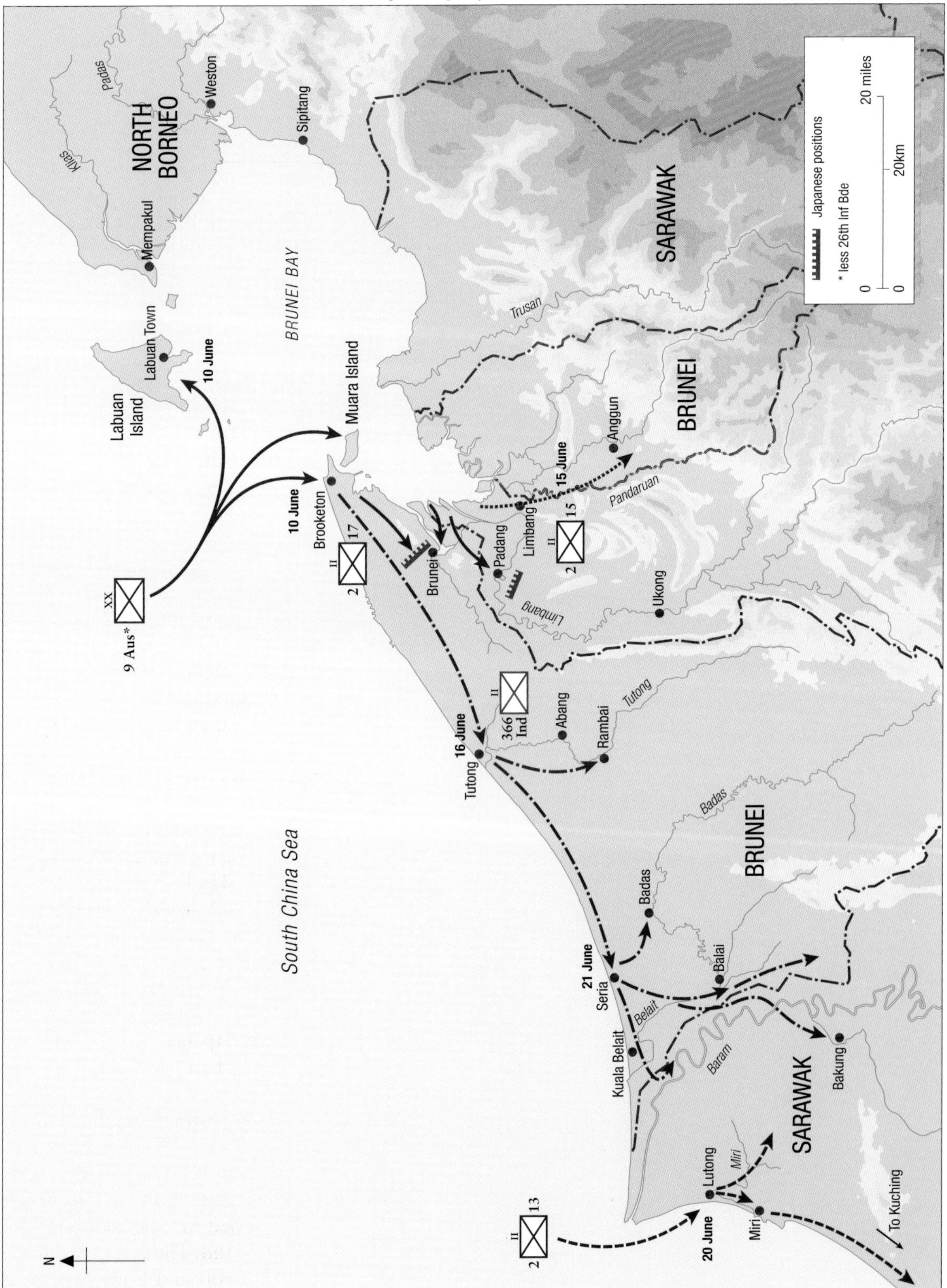

NORTH BORNEO

SARAWAK

BRUNEI

BRUNEI BAY

South China Sea

Padas
Kiau
Weston
Sipitang
Mempakul
Labuan Town
Labuan Island
10 June
Muara Island
Brooketon
10 June
Trusan
Anggun
15 June
Limbang
Pandaruan
15
Ukong
Brunei
Padang
Limbang
Abang
Rambai
Tutong
16 June
Tutong
Badas
Badas
Balai
21 June
Seria
Kuala Belait
Belait
Baram
Bakung
SARAWAK
Lutong
Miri
20 June
Miri
To Kuching

9 Aus* — XX
2/17 — II
2/15 — II
366 Ind — II
2/13 — II

Japanese positions
* less 26th Inf Bde

20 miles
20km
0
0

N

A Matilda II tank of A Sqn, Australian 2/9th Armd Regt on the outskirts of Brooketon in Brunei on 10 June. The squadron was attached to 20th Bde during its invasion of Brunei, and during the landing the squadron operated in direct support of the 2/17th Bttn.

Early on Monday 11 June, the 2/17th led the advance on Brunei town, supported by a troop of Matildas. That morning, the 2/15th on Muara Island also detached a company in landing craft, which ferried it ten miles to the south-west, where it landed at the mouth of the Brunei River to block river access to the town. The company went ashore on the north side of the river mouth at 1500hrs and established its own small perimeter four miles east of Brunei town. Meanwhile, the 2/17th advanced through an area of forest fringed by mangrove swamp, but encountered no opposition.

On Tuesday morning, however, it had its first brush with the enemy. Outside the village of Serusop, three miles to the north of Brunei town, a patrol of the 2/17th engaged a Japanese patrol, which withdrew. Two Indian Army soldiers, who had escaped from a nearby POW camp, confirmed that the Japanese had withdrawn. So, the advance continued, and at 1300hrs,

Despite intelligence reports suggesting the place was occupied, the landing of the 2/15th Bttn on Muara Island in Brunei on 10 June was completely unopposed. Here, infantry of the battalion conduct a sweep of the uninhabited island, supported by American-operated Buffalo LVTs.

Brunei airfield was captured. There the Australians came under fire from Japanese on the higher ground to the south. A company of the 2/17th outflanked and took the position before the battalion dug in for the night, two miles from Brunei town. So far, it had only lost one man killed, and three wounded.

There was some sporadic firing during the night, but at 0900hrs, Windeyer met Lt Col. Broadbent, commander of the 2/17th, and ordered him to press on and capture the town. The advance was unopposed, and by 1300hrs on 13 June, Brunei town was in Australian hands. It appeared that the Japanese 366th Independent Bttn, which had been garrisoning Brunei, had withdrawn towards Limbang. It meant an almost bloodless victory. Next, Windeyer had to secure the rest of the Sultanate, as well as neighbouring Sarawak. That afternoon, he sent half of Lt Col. Grace's 2/15th Bttn west towards the key oil town of Tutong, while other patrols moved south, to contact the retreating Japanese.

Australian soldiers of the 2/17th Bttn examining the bodies of dead Japanese soldiers of the 366th Bttn following a skirmish with a Japanese rear guard just south of Brunei airfield, during 20th Bde's largely unopposed advance on Brunei town on 13 June.

Windeyer had planned to embark the 2/13th again and send it down the coast to Tutong, to secure the oil installations there. However, Wootten envisaged a more ambitious move, and took the battalion under his own command, as well as half of the 2/15th, and ordered them to land 35 miles further west, between Miri and Lutong. This left Windeyer with only half his original force, spread between Tutong and Padang. Still, on 16 June, he sent his two remaining companies of the 2/15th up the Pandaruan River. When they reached Limbang, they found the Japanese had withdrawn. So, it duly became the brigade's new southern base. Friendly Dyaks reported Japanese troops were retreating eastwards, and soon the Australians confirmed this. Over the next few weeks, clashes continued, and on 7 July, a firefight in a swamp ended with around 20 Japanese being killed. They included Maj Sato, the 366th Bttn commander. This effectively ended all organized resistance in the area, allowing Grace to extend his area of control as far as Anggun and Ukong (Okan).

A patrol of the 2/17th Bttn after entering Brunei town on 13 June. The capital of the Sultanate of Brunei was captured without any fighting, as the Japanese withdrew from the city that morning. So, its elegant buildings were largely undamaged.

While the 2/15th was relocating to Limbang, other units were continuing their advance to the west. On 16 June, elements of the 2/17th entered Tutong, then pressed on towards Seria. So far, Japanese opposition had been non-existent. Thirty miles to the west, early on 20 June, the 2/13th Bttn landed near Lutong. This was preceded by air strikes, launched from the newly opened airfields on Labuan, and supported by naval gunnery. Once again, though, the landing was unopposed. Lutong and

Before the landing at nearby Lutong in Eastern Sarawak on 20 June, the harbour town of Miri was bombed by the USAAF, to reduce the town's defences, before the place was captured by the 2/13th Bttn that afternoon. Miri was an important centre of oil production in the region.

its airfield were captured that afternoon, although the nearby oil refinery had been damaged. On Saturday morning, the oilfields at Miri were also captured by the 2/13th, and although these had been set ablaze by the retreating Japanese, Dutch oil workers accompanying the Australians quickly put out the fires. That done, elements of the battalion continued along the coast to Kuching, the capital of Sarawak, 350 miles to the west. The main prize there, apart from the region's administrative centre, was a large POW camp, which was finally liberated by units of the 9th Div on 11 September, almost a month after Japan's surrender.

On the morning of Thursday 21 June, the 2/17th entered Seria unopposed. However, like Miri, the extensive oilfields there had been set ablaze, and the flames from the oil fires rose a thousand feet into the air. This time Australian engineers from the 2/3rd Field Coy attempted to tackle the raging fires, but had limited success until reinforcements arrived to help them, including a Dutch oilfield engineer. Even then, the 37 burning oil wells were only fully extinguished after several weeks of major effort and the arrival of American oil fire experts.

After the capture of most of Brunei and eastern Sarawak, the Australians continued to patrol the hinterland, searching for any remaining pockets of Japanese troops. Here, a patrol from the 2/13th Bttn of 20th Bde sweeps a track near Miri in Sarawak, a few weeks after the official ceasefire.

By this point, apart from minor mopping-up operations, the whole of Brunei had been liberated, as had the Miri–Lutong area of Sarawak. On 24 June, Kuala Belait on the coast was captured, enabling land communications to be established between Lutong and Seria. The 2/13th and 2/17th Bttns then launched patrols further inland, in search of the Japanese,

The numerous oil wells at Seria in Brunei were set ablaze by the retreating Japanese. Here, in a photograph taken from a US Navy PT boat on 28 June, the oilfields are still burning, a week after their capture by 20th Bde's 2/17th Bttn. In the foreground is another PT boat, pictured during a sweep of the Brunei coast.

concentrating on settlements along the Miri, Belait, Badas and Tutong rivers. Landing craft were used, allowing the Australians to penetrate the region's interior quickly. The Australians also made good use of local Dyak guides. Apart from the odd patrol clash, there was little contact with the Japanese, and it became clear that they had withdrawn from the area. What few clashes there were appeared to have been encounters with what amounted to a Japanese rear guard, acting as independent groups of guerrilla fighters.

By this stage of the campaign, as organized resistance ended, the men of the 20th Bde became less concerned with fighting than with supporting the rebuilding of the region. Apart from fighting the oil fires at Seria, the brigade's engineers were fully occupied clearing mines, improving roads and bridges, and rebuilding the infrastructure in Brunei and Sarawak that had been damaged by the retreating Japanese, or by Allied bombs. This work continued until the Japanese surrender in mid-August. By that time, some of the men of the brigade had already been shipped home, as the process of demobilization gathered pace. Casualties in this campaign had been minimal, but the rewards had been significant in terms of territory liberated and the oil and rubber production facilities captured. However, an Allied naval base in Brunei Bay was never established, as the ceasefire ended any need for it.

The Invasion of Labuan

While the Brunei landing got underway, another similar operation was taking place on the north-east side of Brunei Bay. Labuan Island had been part of British North Borneo until it was occupied by the Japanese in February 1942. They duly renamed it Maeda Island, in honour of the Japanese commander in Northern Borneo. They also built two airfields, which they used for reconnaissance operations over the South China Sea. It was these airfields that made Labuan desirable for the Australians. In Allied hands, they could support other operations in Borneo – much like that which had been proposed for Tarakan.

AUSTRALIAN FORCES
9th Inf Div
    24th Inf Bde
        1. 2/28th Inf Bttn
        2. 2/43rd Inf Bttn
        3. 2/11th Commando Sqn
Plus other assets

Note: gridlines are shown at intervals of 1km (0.62 miles)

24 Aus ⊠
PORTER

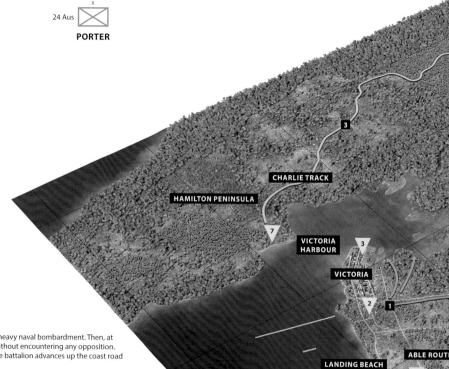

▼ EVENTS

P-Day, Sunday 10 June

1. 0845hrs: Brown Beach is subjected to a heavy naval bombardment. Then, at 0900hrs, the 2/43rd Bttn lands on Brown II without encountering any opposition. At 0920hrs, after securing the beachhead, the battalion advances up the coast road towards the airfield.

2. 0915hrs: The 2/28th Bttn lands on Brown I and secures the beachhead. No opposition is encountered. After securing the beachhead, the battalion advances inland, towards Victoria and Government House.

3. 1015hrs: A Coy of the 2/28th captures Victoria without any opposition. This completes the securing of the beachhead and enables supporting units to begin landing.

4. 1030hrs: The 2/43rd Bttn comes under fire from the direction of Flagstaff Hill. It then bypasses this pocket of resistance and continues its advance towards its primary objective – the airfield.

5. 1045hrs: The remainder of the 2/28th Bttn encounters opposition around Flagstaff Hill, and the junction of Callaghan Road and MacArthur Road. Fighting in this area continues until nightfall, when the Australians break off the action for the night.

6. 1450hrs: The 2/43rd Bttn captures the Japanese aircraft park, then goes on to secure Labuan airfield, again without Japanese opposition, save for harassing fire from mortars and snipers.

7. 1500hrs: The 24th Bde's floating reserve, 2/11th Commando Sqn, lands a troop at 'Hardy' without opposition, and it begins an advance northward up Charlie Track, to clear the Hamilton Peninsula.

P-Day +1, Monday 11 June

8. 0730hrs: The 2/43rd establishes a cordon to the north of the airfield, then moves west to capture the junction of MacArthur Road and Hamilton Road. It discovers the Japanese have now concentrated to the south of the road junction.

9. 0810hrs: The 2/28th Bttn comes under heavy fire as it advances up MacArthur Road. This quickly grows into a major firefight, which lasts for the remainder of the day.

10. 0830hrs: Although Flagstaff Hill is captured, a major pocket of Japanese to the south-west remains. The struggle to subdue it continues until the afternoon, when the Japanese position is finally captured.

11. 1100hrs: The 2/11th Commando Sqn reaches the junction with Hamilton Road, again without encountering any significant opposition.

12. 1330hrs: Elements of the 2/43rd Bttn advance east along MacArthur Road, to secure the secondary airfield at Timbalai, which is captured at dawn the following day.

P-Day +2, Tuesday 12 June

13. 1000hrs: It soon becomes clear that most of the Japanese garrison are entrenched further to the east, on high ground overlooking MacArthur Road. Using tank and artillery support, the 2/43rd Bttn begins to drive in the Japanese perimeter of the Pocket in the face of heavy opposition.

14. 1040hrs: The 2/28th Bttn also presses on the south-eastern perimeter of the Japanese-held high ground, in a series of company-sized assaults. Again, tank, artillery and air support are used extensively to support the attack. The decision is then made to isolate the Pocket, while securing full control of the rest of the island. This is accomplished by the end of 14 June.

P-Day +4, Thursday 14 June.

15. A series of assaults are made to reduce the Japanese perimeter of the Pocket. It is also subjected to heavy artillery bombardment and air attacks. However, the Pocket is only fully subdued on 21 June. This effectively ends all Japanese resistance on Labuan.

THE INVASION OF LABUAN, BORNEO, 1–21 JUNE 1945

The second phase of Operation *Oboe* saw Australian landings in northern Borneo, at Brunei and on Labuan, an island at the head of Brunei Bay. Although the initial landing on Labuan of 10 June was unopposed, Japanese resistance mounted as the invaders pushed inland towards the island's main airfield and Government House. While the airfield was captured relatively quickly, fighting around Flagstaff Hill lasted into the following day. Then, as one Australian battalion pushed west across the island to secure the second smaller airfield, Japanese resistance coalesced further south, four miles north of Victoria, in a hilltop position the Australians called the 'Pocket'. It was eventually subdued on 21 June, after some bitter and costly fighting, leaving Labuan firmly under Allied control.

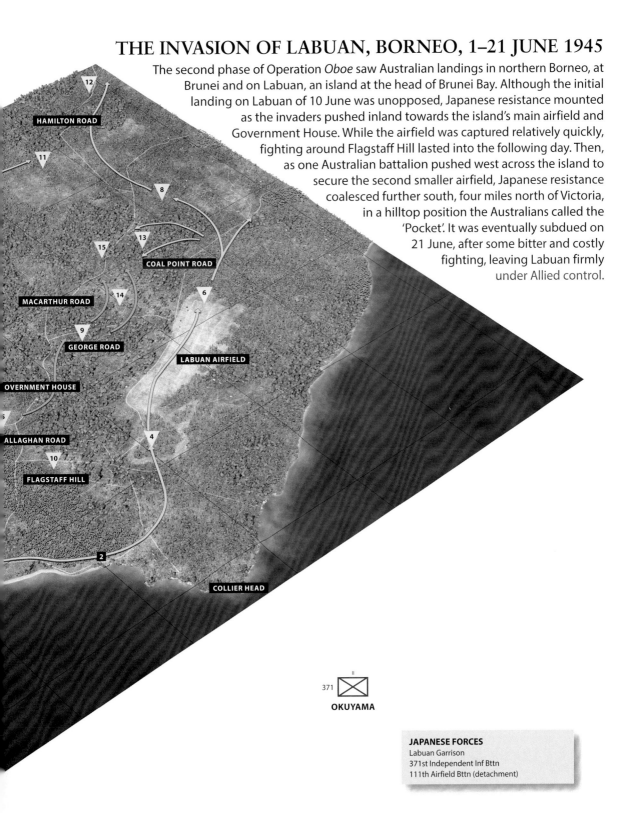

HAMILTON ROAD

COAL POINT ROAD

MACARTHUR ROAD

GEORGE ROAD

LABUAN AIRFIELD

OVERNMENT HOUSE

ALLAGHAN ROAD

FLAGSTAFF HILL

COLLIER HEAD

371 [⊠] OKUYAMA

JAPANESE FORCES
Labuan Garrison
371st Independent Inf Bttn
111th Airfield Bttn (detachment)

A company command group of 2/43rd Bttn pictured on Labuan on 26 June, during the sweep of the northern part of the island for any remaining Japanese troops. Five days earlier, the bulk of the Japanese garrison had been overrun in the Pocket.

Labuan, June 1945

The invasion of Labuan was carried out by Brig Selwyn Porter's Australian 24th Inf Bde, part of the 9th Inf Div. Porter's command only had two infantry battalions, the 2/28th and the 2/43rd, as his third battalion was held as a corps reserve. Still, these were supported by the 25-pdrs of the 2/12th Field Regt, the 2/11th Commando Sqn and detachments drawn from the 2/9th Armd Regt, the 2/2nd Machine Gun Bttn and divisional engineers.

The plan called for an amphibious landing at 0915hrs beside Victoria, the main settlement on the island. This landing area, designated Brown Beach, would be made on a two-battalion front, with the 2/43rd on the right and the 2/28th on the left. The commandos would be held as a floating reserve. The 2/28th was to capture Victoria and secure the beachhead, while the 2/43rd would take Labuan airfield, two miles to the north-east. The brigade would then capture the island's secondary airfield on its western coast and clear the remainder of the island. Labuan was just under 12 miles long and 6½ miles across at its widest point, and the garrison was a single Japanese battalion. This therefore was considered eminently achievable, particularly as the attackers would have the support of a powerful naval force.

At 0845hrs that morning, R Adm Berkey's three light cruisers began their bombardment of the shore behind Brown Beach, immediately to the east of Victoria. Once the landing craft began their approach, the bombardment would move inland. On schedule, Lt Col. Norman's 2/28th Bttn stepped ashore on Brown Beach. There was no enemy opposition, and the beach itself was quickly secured. Moments later,

On the afternoon of 10 June, once the main bridgehead on Labuan was secure, Brig Porter ordered his reserve of the 2/11th Commando Sqn to land a troop on the far side of the harbour on the Hamilton Peninsula. Here, commandos disembark there from an LCI.

over to the right, the leading waves of Lt Col. Mervyn Jeanes' 2/43rd Bttn also reached the beach. By then, the naval bombardment had shifted to the area between Victoria and Flagstaff Hill, a mile north.

Once ashore, a company of the 2/28th was sent to the left to secure Victoria, while two more advanced northwards towards a crossroads at the foot of Flagstaff Hill. Norman kept his fourth company in reserve. It was found that the town had been abandoned by the Japanese, and the company there joined the battalion reserve. On their right, the 2/43rd also began its own advance on a two-company frontage, with its right flank anchored on the coast road, codenamed 'Able Route'. Just after 1030hrs, its left-hand company came under small-arms fire from the direction of Flagstaff Hill. Lt Col. Simpson ordered the company to avoid contact, and his men bypassed the Japanese. His mission, after all, was to capture the airfield.

Men of the 2/43rd Bttn embarked on an American-operated Buffalo LVT during the approach of the first wave to Brown II Beach on the morning of 10 June. Each LVT was designed to carry up to 24 passengers, but due to a shortage of LVTs during *Oboe 6*, four extra men were embarked in them during the landing.

A few minutes later, at 1045hrs, the right-hand leading company of the 2/28th Bttn also came under fire from the south slopes of the same hill. Capt Lushington, who led the company, ignored the firing and continued towards the hill's summit. While his company deployed there, someone raised a British Union flag on the hill's flagstaff, which rather surprisingly had withstood the naval bombardment. Then, on reaching the crossroads of Callaghan Road and MacArthur Road, the left-hand company of the battalion came under fire from the north-east – the area around Government House. This time there was no avoiding the enemy, and a major firefight developed, increasing in ferocity as the day progressed.

Over to the east though, the 2/43rd was still advancing. It followed Able Route as it led northwards, accompanied by a troop of Matilda tanks. There was no real opposition to speak of, apart from a two-man Japanese

A corporal from the 2/43rd Bttn provides cover during the battalion's advance on Labuan airfield on 10 June. This section leader, armed with an Owen sub-machine gun, is overlooking the Japanese aircraft dispersal bays, on the southern side of the airfield.

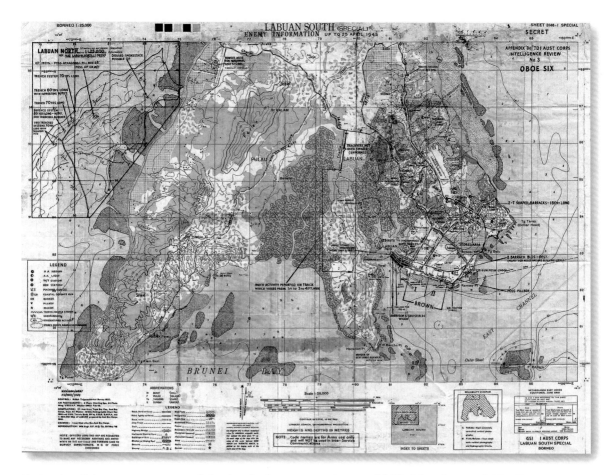

The invasion of Labuan was preceded by extensive intelligence-gathering efforts, both from reconnaissance aircraft and from reconnaissance landing parties. This is the result, a detailed map of southern Labuan, showing the Japanese positions and defences around Victoria and Labuan airfield.

patrol, both of whom were shot and killed by the roadside. Progress was only slowed when local refugees began filtering past them down the road, desperate to pass through Allied lines. This was the situation at noon, when an unexpected group of visitors appeared at Lt Col. Jeanes' command post. Gen MacArthur and Lt Gen Morshead suddenly arrived, accompanied by press photographers. Having watched the landing, they then came ashore to see the operation for themselves. The high-ranking visitors were given a briefing by the colonel, and contented, their cavalcade drove back towards the beachhead.

By 1400hrs, the 2/43rd had reached the aircraft park on the southern side of the airfield. A few small patrol skirmishes took place, but Simpson's cautious advance continued, and shortly before 1500hrs the airfield itself was captured. Meanwhile, the firefight near Government House was still in full flow, but Norman had reinforced his leading companies, and had overcome a few Japanese pockets behind his front line, which ran from Flagstaff Hill

The initial landing on Labuan's Brown Beach was carried out by small landing craft and Buffalo LVTs, carrying the first wave of two Australian battalions. The LCVPs (or Higgins boats) pictured here could each carry up to 36 men, and during their approach they were supported by larger LCIs armed with rockets, mortars and light guns. One of these is shown on the left.

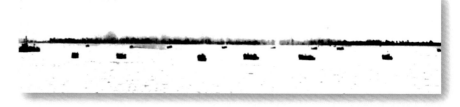

to the crossroads, and then to the south-west, until it reached the shore. However, this was just a mile from the beachhead, where the brigade was busily landing supplies. The fighting around the crossroads continued throughout the afternoon, with all attempts to oust the Japanese defenders thwarted by Japanese machine guns that covered the crossroads. Even tank support did little to improve the situation for the 2/28th, as mines and swampy ground greatly restricted their use.

Once his two battalions were established ashore, Brig Porter planned to land Maj Clements' commandos on the Hamilton Peninsula, at the western side of Victoria Harbour. There, Charlie Track led northwards from Hardy's Landing to reach the Hamilton Road – the route that bisected the island from east to west. The aim was to come round the back of the Japanese garrison fighting near Government House and cut off their line of retreat. However, locals told the Australians that there were no Japanese on the peninsula. So, Porter decided to land just a single troop of 50 commandos.

Australian infantry of the 2/43rd Bttn disembarking from an LST onto the Labuan invasion beach on 10 May. While these could carry up to 20 tanks – a full squadron – they were also used to transport up to 180 infantry or up to five smaller LCAs.

They would move up the peninsula and take up a blocking position astride Hamilton Road.

The fighting around Government House petered out as the sun set at around 1800hrs. At 2200hrs, Porter ordered the 2/43rd to move up from the airport, to secure the junction of the MacArthur Road and Hamilton Road. There, Jeanes' troops would link up with the commando troop a few hundred yards further west. Porter, though, did not know where all the island's Japanese garrisons were. So far, the only major Japanese concentration was facing the 2/28th. At dawn on 11 June, two companies of the 2/43rd led the advance towards the road junction, accompanied by tanks, and easily brushed aside any Japanese outposts.

To the south, Lt Col. Norman moved two companies up Able Route to outflank the Japanese positions from the east. They ran into Japanese troops in the wooded ground to the east of Government House. Shortly after 0800hrs, the rest of the battalion tried to resume its advance up MacArthur Road from the south, but it was pinned down by heavy fire. Another firefight erupted around Flagstaff Hill, while more pockets of Japanese were still holding out at the crossroads. The fight to subdue them continued for the remainder of the day, until the Japanese outposts were finally overrun just before dusk. Still, better progress was made to the north of the hill, as B Coy pushed the enemy back from the woods and closed in on Government House from the east.

Meanwhile, the commando troop that had advanced up the Hamilton Peninsula reached the Hamilton Road intersection at 1100hrs. They reported that the area was clear of the enemy, with only small groups of Japanese spotted on the road. By then, the 2/43rd had captured the road junction 1,200yds to the east of the commandos, and so Lt Col. Jeanes detached a company to move along Hamilton Road to the north-east, towards the secondary Japanese airfield at Timbalai, three miles away. It reached the airfield just before dawn the next day and captured it without any opposition.

By then, it was clear that the bulk of Labuan's Japanese garrison was concentrated in the area east of MacArthur Road, between the two Australian battalions. Rather than launch an all-out attack, Porter ordered his battalion commanders to pin the enemy, while his artillery, which had been deployed ashore, pounded the Japanese positions. So, Tuesday 12 June was a day of company-sized probes. With tank support, the 2/28th advanced 500yds up MacArthur Road, despite mines and IEDs blocking the road. To the north, the 2/43rd did the same, and by the afternoon, it was clear, apart from a few stragglers, that the Japanese had withdrawn to the high ground to the east of the road.

This meant that the Australians had encircled the Japanese on three sides. The mangrove swamps and wetlands to the west were impassable. Therefore, the Australians dubbed this position the 'Pocket', an area just 1,200yds long and 600yds wide. Subduing it became Porter's primary objective. Over the next few days, the artillery bombardment and airstrikes continued, as the Australian battalions strengthened their encirclement. Meanwhile, patrols from the 2/43rd and the 2/11th Commando Sqn ranged across the rest of the island. Several stray Japanese servicemen were discovered, and either captured or killed. By the evening of 14 June, it was even clearer that all the remaining Japanese troops on Labuan were concentrated in the Pocket.

The Japanese position was a strong one. With mangrove swamps on its western side and marshland to the south and east, the avenues of attack were limited to the north, where the approaches were dominated by 'Lyon Ridge', or the east, where a small track crossed the band of marshy ground between the lines to climb onto 'Lushington Ridge'. Both had been named after company commanders of the 2/28th. Linking the two of them, like the spine of the letter 'E', was 'Norman Ridge', named after the battalion commander. The central prong of the 'E' was called 'Eastman Spur', after another company commander. All this high ground was clad in woods and

The small town of Victoria on Labuan was badly damaged during the air attacks and naval bombardment that preceded the Australian landings on 10 June. Its ruins were quickly secured by the 2/28th Bttn after it landed a few hundred yards from it on Brown I Beach. This shows the north side of the town as it appeared that afternoon.

A patrol made up of men from C Coy, 2/43rd Bttn, searching the remoter parts of Labuan for any remaining Japanese there. When this was taken on 15 June, ten days after the landing on the island, almost all of the Japanese garrison was concentrated inside the Pocket, but a handful of troops still remained at large elsewhere on the island.

scrub, but the near-constant artillery bombardment gradually denuded the area of its cover.

Porter began by probing the defences. On 14 June, a company of the 2/28th attacked the Pocket in the early afternoon, preceded by an artillery bombardment, but it was forced to withdraw in the face of heavy enemy fire. The next morning, a commando patrol discovered that the track on the northern side of Lyon Ridge was suitable for tanks, if a large bomb crater could be filled in first. So, at 0845hrs on Saturday 16 June, Maj Lyon's A Coy of the 2/28th advanced up the track, supported by a troop of Matildas. A bulldozer was used to fill in the crater, which allowed the armour to reach the crest of Lyon Ridge at 1020hrs. However, heavy fire from Eastman Spur to the south prevented A Coy from advancing further. By noon, though, Norman had established his battalion command post on the ridge and was calling down artillery fire on the spur.

When Lyon was wounded, Capt Eastman took the lead, and at noon his company moved down into the dip between the ridge and the spur, and then up its side, with a fresh troop of Matildas leading the way. One tank was disabled by an IED, and another bogged down, but by early afternoon, the Australians had established themselves on Eastman Ridge. That though, was as far as they could manage that day. Having lost five men killed and 23 wounded, Norman intended to avoid further casualties. Instead, what was left of the Pocket would be pounded by artillery, while the 2/28th prepared for a final assault. For the next three days, artillery battered Norman and Lushington Ridges, while on the Monday morning the newly arrived heavy cruiser HMAS *Shropshire* added the weight of its 8in guns to the barrage.

The 2/12th Field Regt fired 140 tons of shells at the Japanese position that week, making it one of the heaviest artillery barrages of the campaign. On Tuesday 19 June, a platoon-sized probe suggested that the Japanese were less able to defend their ground than before, thanks to casualties and damage to weapons. Nevertheless, the relentless bombardment continued, and on the Wednesday, air strikes were launched for good measure. By then,

Porter and Norman agreed the enemy had been battered sufficiently to give a final assault every chance of success. So, a two-company attack would be launched on Thursday morning, 21 June.

However, at 0430hrs, the Japanese struck first. Completely unexpectedly, a sortie by 50 Japanese soldiers ran amok inside the bridgehead and other rear areas, having bypassed the encirclement by wading through the mangrove swamps. A POW cage was stormed, and a camp of American boat crews attacked. An Australian and three Americans were killed, but quick-thinking by non-combatants held the attackers in check until reinforcements could arrive. In all, some 32 Japanese troops were killed in the sortie. Another group managed to reach Labuan airfield, and there, a bayonet attack against the engineers of the 2/7th Field Coy saw another 11 Japanese killed, for the loss of one Australian. After the firefight, Norman sent a company to scour the beachhead in case any more Japanese raiders remained.

This, however, did not delay the long-awaited Australian attack. At 1000hrs, Capt Lushington's C Coy of the 2/28th advanced up the track through the marsh to attack Lushington Ridge from the east, under cover of an artillery bombardment. At the same time, Maj Lyon's A Coy attacked from Eastman Spur. Both companies were supported by a troop of Matilda tanks, while A Coy was also joined by a troop of 'Frogs' – Matilda tanks equipped with flamethrowers. This time, Japanese resistance was lacklustre, and so by 1130hrs, Lushington had cleared the ridge named after him. Norman then ordered C Coy to pause, to avoid any friendly fire incidents. It was just as well, as the Frogs were unstoppable, and with a combination of these flamethrowers, the close-support Matildas and the infantry of A Coy, the attackers swept everything before them.

It seemed to the attackers that their Japanese opponents were dazed by the days of shelling they had endured. They were unable to put up any effective resistance, and by early afternoon, the Pocket had been overrun. In all, around 60 Japanese troops were killed that day, while the bodies of another 40 were also found, having died during the bombardment. Later, another 77 bodies were found in shallow graves. Only six men were taken prisoner. In effect, the whole Pocket garrison of around 250 men had been wiped out. Later, the Australians reckoned only 11 Japanese troops were unaccounted for on Labuan and were probably either dead or in hiding. In all, some 389 Japanese soldiers were killed on the island, and 11 taken prisoner. For its part, the Australian brigade lost 34 men killed, and 93 more wounded.

The invasion of Labuan was accounted a clear success for the Australians. Equally impressive was the speedy repair of the two airfields. On the day after the capture of Labuan airfield, engineers were brought in to repair it, and by 16 June, it was deemed to be operational. Aircraft based there

A Matilda Frog – the flamethrower version of the British-built infantry support tank of 1st Armd Regt, pictured in operation with the 2/10th Bttn on 3 July, during the battalion's advance up a track in the high ground to the east of Balikpapan. These were fearsome and highly potent weapons.

were therefore able to support Australian operations in Brunei, Sarawak and North Borneo. This, after all, was the main reason Labuan had been attacked – to serve as a static aircraft carrier for the Allies. Thanks to some hard fighting by Porter's brigade, this air support was available within a week of the landing.

North Borneo

By 16 June, Maj Gen Wootten felt that as the Borneo and Labuan operations had been successful, it was time to expand his division's operations. His next objective was the British dependency of North

Civilians on Labuan, pictured with Australian soldiers six days after the landing there. During the initial landing on 10 June, the advancing Australians were passed by large numbers of refugees, attempting to flee from the Japanese. Afterwards, their liberators had to feed and house much of the island's population.

Borneo. There, by landing troops on the eastern side of Brunei Bay, he could conduct a reconnaissance, and probe towards the important regional town of Beaufort. This would precede an attack by the 24th Inf Bde. Wootten's divisional reserve consisted of Lt Col. Scott's 2/32nd Bttn and the 2/12th Commando Sqn. These would spearhead this reconnaissance. So, a week after the landings at Brunei and Labuan, the invasion got underway. It began modestly, with detachments of Scott's battalion put ashore at Weston. These patrols found that the area was clear of Japanese troops, and the following day the rest of the battalion was landed there. Weston was not an ideal bridgehead, as it was surrounded by mangrove swamps and marshes, with a single track and a narrow-gauge railway leading inland from it. Nevertheless, for the time being, it would serve Scott's needs.

By the end of that Sunday, Australian patrols had reached Lingkungan, and the following day Maraba was entered, four miles east of the Weston beachhead. The only sign of the enemy was a brief clash with a Japanese patrol outside Lingkungan. Meanwhile, on Wootten's orders, another landing took place further north up the coast, at Mempakul Beach, near the North Borneo village of Menumbok. This too, was undefended, and two companies of Lt Col. Jeanes' 2/43rd Bttn, fresh from Labuan, established themselves there on Tuesday 19 June. It was their second amphibious landing in just over a week. Their objective was to advance northwards up the coast towards Cape Nosong, to clear it of Japanese, and so make it available for the landing of supplies to support the Australian advance.

Meanwhile at Lingkungan, locals told Scott that around 800–1,000 Japanese soldiers were in the area, but were withdrawing towards the village of Bukau, three miles north-east of Maraba. Presumably, they would be heading towards Beaufort. Minor clashes over the next few days helped confirm these reports. By then, though, the fighting in Labuan had ended, and the 2/17th Field Regt was being sent to support the advance in North Borneo. So too were Brig Porter and his staff, and the 2/28th Bttn, after its clearing of the Pocket. Porter saw that there were two main routes to Beaufort. One was along the narrow-gauge railway line, which ran north-east from Weston and on to Beaufort by way of Lumadan. The other was

AUSTRALIAN AMBUSH NEAR BEAUFORT, NORTH BORNEO (PP.68–69)

Oboe 6 was the codename for the Australian landings in North Borneo. Its objective was securing Brunei Bay for use as an Allied forward naval base, and to capture the oil and rubber production facilities in the area. On 10 June, brigade-sized landings were made around Brunei, which was taken with minimal resistance, and on the small island of Labuan, which was secured 11 days later. Then, on 17 June, the Australians landed near Weston in North Borneo, on the north-east side of Brunei Bay, and advanced by various routes towards the Japanese stronghold of Beaufort. This phase of the campaign saw fierce fighting before the surviving defenders were driven back into the jungle. Low-key skirmishes continued until the ceasefire in mid-August.

This shows one of the many skirmishes during the advance on Beaufort. The 2/32nd Bttn advanced up the Padas River, using a mixture of landing craft for the main force, led by advance parties moving along the riverbanks and native tracks. The Japanese continued to harry the advancing Australians, and skirmishes and firefights took place. This depicts one of them, when an Australian scouting force encountered a Japanese boat patrol on the Padas River near the village of Gadong. The Australian section, led by a corporal (**1**), lay in wait for the Japanese (**2**), who used local sampans fitted with outboard motors to patrol the river. In this encounter, the squad-sized Japanese patrol returning upstream was accompanied by a Japanese officer (**3**), charged with determining the location of the enemy's forward positions. The ambushers included a Bren gun team (**4**), which provided the section's main firepower, supported by a rifle team armed with SMLE Mark III rifles, and, in this case, an Owen sub-machine gun (**5**). At this point, the Padas River, flowing from Japanese-held Beaufort to Australian-held Weston on the coast, was around 120yds wide. The southern bank (**6**) of the river also contained another Australian scouting patrol.

The conquest of North Borneo, June–August 1945

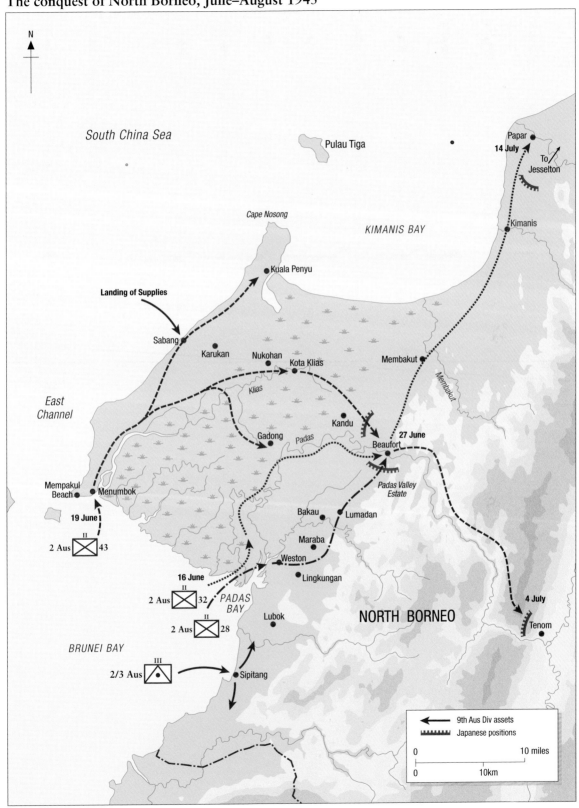

South China Sea

Pulau Tiga

Papar

14 July

To Jesselton

Kimanis

Cape Nosong

KIMANIS BAY

N

Kuala Penyu

Landing of Supplies

Sabang

Karukan

Nukohan

Kota Klias

Membakut

Klias

Membakut

East Channel

Gadong

Padas

Kandu

27 June

Beaufort

Padas Valley Estate

Mempakul Beach

Menumbok

19 June

2 Aus | II | 43

Bakau

Lumadan

Maraba

Weston

16 June

2 Aus | II | 32

PADAS BAY

Lingkungan

Lubok

NORTH BORNEO

2 Aus | II | 28

4 July

Tenom

BRUNEI BAY

2/3 Aus | III

Sipitang

9th Aus Div assets

Japanese positions

0   10 miles

0   10km

the Padas River, which entered Brunei Bay on the north side of Padas Bay, opposite Weston.

So, he decided to land the 2/28th at Weston, to take over the advance towards Lumadan. Scott's battalion would be ferried across the bay to the mouth of the Padas. From there it would move upriver in landing crafts, preceded by patrols advancing up the riverbanks. As Porter put it, he 'decided to conform to local practice and travel by water'. For this mission though, the LCMs were modified to carry 3in mortars and machine guns, and were protected by sandbag bulwarks. Each landing craft could transport a platoon. As the probe towards Beaufort began, the Australians made good use of the locals for information on Japanese outposts and patrols. On the Padas, the leading elements of the 2/32nd reached the village of Gadong and established its battalion base there.

Although Japanese riverine patrols were encountered, there was no sign of any real Japanese presence in the area. Lt Col. Scott therefore decided to press on towards Beaufort. Meanwhile, to the north, the 2/43rd supported by the 2/11th Commando Sqn advanced up the coast north of the Klias River, while a company also steamed up the river itself, to support the flank of the 2/32nd at Gadong. It reached Kota Klias, ten miles north of Beaufort, before locals warned them that the Japanese had outposts nearby. To the north, the rest of the force encountered nothing more than occasional Japanese patrols along the coast, and by 23 June, it had reached Sabang and Karukan, where it was reinforced from the sea by the remainder of the battalion. Four days later, the commandos reached Kuala Penyu, below Cape Nosong. So, with the whole coastal area secure, the 2/43rd, which was around Kota Klias, was free to move on Beaufort.

While two companies of the 2/28th remained in the Weston and Lingkungan area to protect the bridgehead there, the remaining two battalions led by Maj Jackson advanced up the railway towards Beaufort. By 25 June, it had passed through Lumadan, and was in the Padas Valley Estate, encountering little more than the occasional Japanese outpost or patrol. It was clear that the Japanese had withdrawn to Beaufort, and were preparing to defend the small town. They were all part of Maj Gen Taijiro Akashi's 56th Independent Mixed Bde, the formation charged with the defence of the whole region, but only elements of it were in Beaufort. These included the 368th Independent Inf Bttn, together with machine gun, engineer and signals troops, but these units were all well under strength. Their numbers were estimated at around 800–1,000 men, although many of these were in poor health. They also lacked artillery support. As such, the Australians had the edge in both numbers and firepower.

By 26 June, Porter had the major portion of two of his battalions deployed within a few miles of Beaufort. The 2/28th was still too far to the south to intervene. Porter's headquarters had moved up the Padas River, and was established to the south-east of Kandu, next to the 2/17th Field Regt, which had also been moved upriver by landing craft, then emplaced a few miles to the west of Beaufort. Australian patrols determined that the bulk of Akashi's force was deployed to the south of the Padas River, to defend the town from an attack up the line of the railway leading from Weston. The Japanese also held the heights immediately to the east of the town.

On 26 June, Porter ordered the 2/32nd to advance towards the spur of high ground to the south of Beaufort, which ran north to the river and overlooked the town. The 2/43rd would also move closer to Beaufort, on the north bank of the river, and from there it would launch a drive to take the lower slopes of Mount Lawley, the high ground overlooking Beaufort from the east. It would then climb the heights from the north. The attack was scheduled to begin the following afternoon. That afternoon, the 2/32nd Bttn advanced to the south of the river, moving towards its start line for the main attack the following day.

By nightfall, it was deployed on the high ground just over half a mile west of the wooded ridge held by the Japanese, and just over a mile

from Beaufort station, on the far bank of the river. Meanwhile, the 2/43rd also advanced up the north bank of the Padas and was in position a mile to the north-west of the town, on the opposite side of the river from the 2/32nd. During the morning of Wednesday 27 June, the Australian artillery pounded the Japanese high ground on both sides of the town. The main attack began at 1400hrs. Two companies of the 2/32nd attacked the Japanese-held ridge from the north-west, along the south side of the river, and from the south-west, after a flank march to the south. Opposition was light, which suggested most of the Japanese had withdrawn into the town.

On 17 June, the 2/32nd Bttn of 9th Inf Div's reserve was landed at Weston in North Borneo by American-crewed Buffalo LVTs. The landing was unopposed, and the Australians quickly established a secure beachhead, as part of the division's drive to liberate North Borneo.

The 2/43rd launched its attack at the same time, with two companies bypassing the town, to pass its northern fringe through orchards to reach the high ground beyond it from the west. Japanese outposts north of the town were taken easily, and by mid-afternoon, the battalion had established a foothold on the lower slopes of Mount Lawley. There though, Japanese fire was heavier, and so Lt Col. Jeanes had his men outflank the enemy to the north-east, before climbing the forest-clad mountain. Shortly after nightfall, the Australians reached the summit, and then established themselves below it, on the flank of the Japanese positions. That night, the Japanese counter-attacked, and one of the battalion's forward companies was cut off. The Australians held their ground, but the Japanese attacks continued well into the following morning. At times, these resulted in fierce hand-to-hand fighting.

As the 2/43rd was establishing itself on Mount Lawley, over to the west of the town, the 2/32nd consolidated its position on the ridge on the south side of the river. A pocket of Japanese remained on that bank, close to the river, but Lt Col. Scott managed to bypass them, and after fording the river, a company entered Beaufort, and captured the railway station. On Thursday morning, the fighting resumed, but by then Porter had been reinforced by a troop of tanks, which were landed from LCTs on the north bank of the Padas River. However, engineers still had to clear the western approaches to the town of mines and IEDs, and this work was still being carried out when the Japanese withdrew the following evening.

On 28 June, heavy fighting resumed on the wooded slopes to the east of the town, but Jeanes' companies managed to edge forward, supported by artillery barrages. The Japanese were well dug in and the terrain with its forested gullies and slopes favoured the defender. Dislodging the Japanese therefore proved difficult. Still, a series of aggressive assaults, close artillery and mortar support helped turn the tide. Capt Pollock's company of the 2/43rd eventually found itself overlooking the south-east side of the town, where the Australians saw bodies of Japanese troops withdrawing along the road that skirted the north bank of the river. Not only were they able to witness the Japanese withdrawal from Beaufort, but they were able to harass the enemy as they retreated. The Australian artillery did the same.

Dawn on Friday revealed an empty town. The battle for Beaufort was over, and Porter ordered his weary men to consolidate their grip on the town, and then send patrols in pursuit of the retreating Japanese. In all, 93 Japanese soldiers were killed during this engagement, and two more taken prisoner. Australian losses were more modest, 7 men killed and 38 wounded. The fall of Beaufort left the Australians in control of a large swathe of North Borneo. After bringing up supplies, using jeeps running along the narrow-gauge railway, the brigade then fanned out to the east. Beaufort, though, proved to be the last major battle in the region. The 2/32nd pursued the retreating Japanese up the railway line to the north-east, and on 14 July, it captured Papar, 30 miles beyond Beaufort. Meanwhile, the 2/43rd advanced up the Padas River, and took Tenom, which was linked to Beaufort by another small railway. The Japanese were still a threat, but never took the offensive. Minor clashes continued, though, until the ceasefire of 15 August. Essentially, North Borneo was securely in Allied hands, and work to restore a civil administration was well under way by the time the fighting ended.

BALIKPAPAN

Once the Australians were firmly established ashore in North Borneo, attention again shifted to the island's eastern coast, but this time just over 300 miles south of Tarakan. The final part of Operation *Oboe* to be enacted was *Oboe 2*, the capture of the oil port of Balikpapan. Not only would this see the largest amphibious operation undertaken by the Australians, but it would also be the last significant amphibious landing of the war. This was also the first attack on the mainland of Dutch Borneo. Balikpapan was the largest centre of oil production in Borneo, and at its height in 1943, it was producing over 50,000 tons of oil a year, all of which was fuelling the Japanese war effort. Although Allied bombing had reduced this considerably, Balikpapan remained an important strategic objective.

The port lay on the east shore of Balikpapan Bay, an inlet on the Borneo side of the Macassar Strait. To the south was Klandasan, the town's European suburb – or it was before its inhabitants were executed by the Japanese in early 1942. It faced the open sea, and between the two lay a steep ridge, with oil tanks and a cracking plant, used to break down oil into lighter products such as propane. The narrow coastal plain ran eastwards from Klandasan, and a road beside it linked the port to a pair of Japanese airfields, at Sepinggan and Manggar. Further inland, the ground rose steeply, and much of it was clad in forest, with little in the way of roads or tracks. However, one metalled road ran inland from Klandasan and Balikpapan, and led on to the oilfields of Sambodja and Sangasangga (now Sanga Sanga), to the north-east.

The invasion of Balikpapan, July 1945

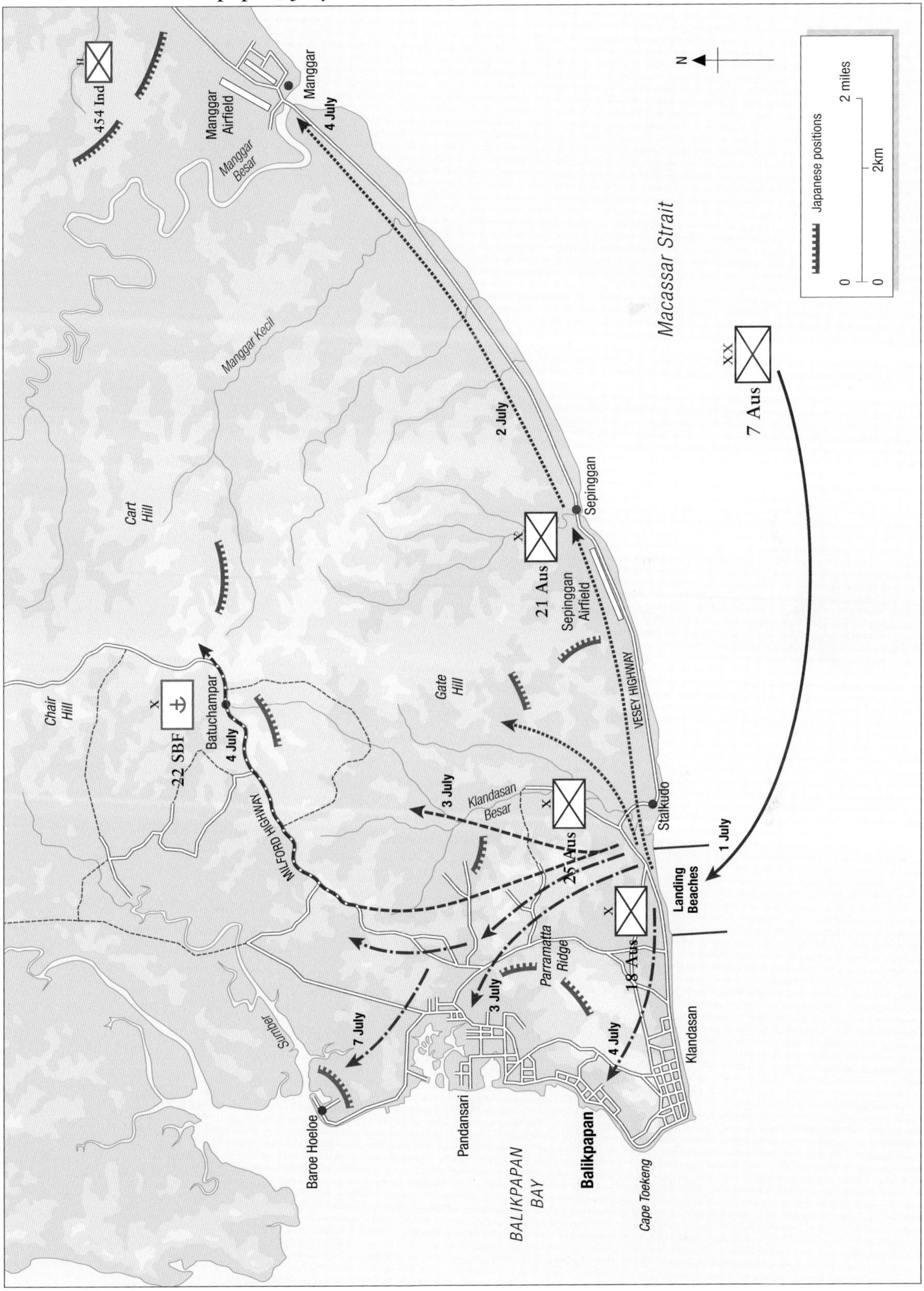

454 Ind

Manggar
Manggar Airfield
Manggar Besar
4 July

Manggar Kecil

2 July

Sepinggan
21 Aus
Sepinggan Airfield

Cart Hill

Gate Hill

N

Macassar Strait

Japanese positions

2 miles

2km

0   0

XX
7 Aus

1 July

Chair Hill

22 SBF

Batuchampar
4 July

MILFORD HIGHWAY

3 July
Klandasan Besar

25 Aus

Stalkudo

VESEY HIGHWAY

Landing Beaches

Parramatta Ridge

18 Aus
Klandasan

Sumber

7 July

3 July

4 July

Baroe Hoeloe

Pandansari

Balikpapan

Cape Toekeng

BALIKPAPAN BAY

Being such an important objective, Balikpapan was well defended, with around 10,000 Japanese troops stationed in the area. However, many of these manned static coastal defences and anti-aircraft batteries, or were armed construction workers. The fighting core of the garrison was the 71st Mixed Independent Bde and the 22nd Naval Special Base Force. Together, these formations amounted to around 3,900 Japanese troops. The most feasible landing area was to the east of Klandasan, but this was covered by coastal batteries at Klandasan and Cape Toekeng, and by emplacements on the high ground overlooking the coastal plain. The beach running from Klandasan to Manggar was protected by mines and underwater obstacles, an anti-tank ditch above the beach itself, and a line of bunkers and concrete pillboxes. An assault on Balikpapan was not going to be easy.

Pre-Invasion Operations

The task of capturing Balikpapan was given to Maj Gen Edward Milford's 7th Australian Inf Div. This was a veteran division, having seen extensive action in North Africa and in New Guinea. Milford had three infantry brigades at his disposal, the 18th, 21st and 25th, and a range of supporting formations, including armour, engineer, artillery and logistics units, and beach landing groups. At this stage of the war, and after the experience of Tarakan, the emphasis was on reducing Australian casualties. So, extensive use would be made of Allied warships for naval gunfire support, and aircraft of the USAAF and RAAF, operating from airfields in the Philippines, particularly in the Sulu Archipelago. The Australian planners also factored in extensive minesweeping work off the landing beaches. This in turn required their protection, which involved neutralizing the Japanese coastal guns using airstrikes and naval bombardment.

Planning was carried out by I Corps staff on Morotai, supported by American planners and advisors from late April on. After weighing up the options, Morshead and his staff selected landing on the coast immediately east of Klandasan, on a 2,000yd front. As this area was well defended, the amphibious landing would be preceded by extensive naval bombardment and air strikes. These airstrikes began on 10 June, and continued for 20 days, until the actual landing, P-Day, which was scheduled for Sunday 1 July 1945. On 15 June, the minesweeping operation began, and it too continued until the eve of P-Day. This dangerous work was vital to the success of *Oboe 2*, and so the minesweepers were heavily supported by Allied warships of the US 7th Fleet. An attack by Japanese torpedo boats on 24 June was beaten off, but during the two weeks of minesweeping, three minesweepers were lost. Despite all this, their mission was a success.

Australian troops from 2/12th Bttn, 18th Bde, 7th Inf Div, form part of the first wave of the landing on Red Beach near Balikpapan on 1 July. They were transported inshore by Buffalo LVTs of the US 672nd Amphibious Tractor Bttn. The smoke behind the beach comes from a burning oil pipeline.

One of the keys to Australian success during the Borneo campaign was the availability of fire support to the infantry. Here, during the advance towards Balikpapan on 1 July, a forward observer calls for fire support from the warships lying in the Macassar Strait.

So too was the destruction or at least neutralizing of the Japanese shore defences, including the coastal gun batteries by naval gunfire and aerial bombing. Over 7,000 tons of bombs were dropped on them, as well as 38,000 naval shells. Also hit were the two airfields in the area, and the beach defences and defensive positions further inland that were identified by the planners. To help them, covert reconnaissance parties were landed from submarines in the area during the weeks preceding the landing to gain a clear picture of the landing beaches and the hinterland. Other parties were parachuted in to link up with local guerrilla groups and gain further intelligence while operating with them. During the week before the landing, American underwater demolition teams were sent in to clear paths through the underwater beach defences – much as the Australian sappers had done at Tarakan. Once all these vital preliminary tasks were completed, Morshead gave the order that set the whole amphibious operation in motion.

A 4.2in heavy mortar manned by a crew of the 2/2nd Anti-Tank Regt, firing in support of the 2/10th Bttn during their advance on Parramatta on 1 July. As anti-tank guns were of little use in the Pacific, the regiment was re-equipped with other more useful support weapons – heavy mortars and 75mm pack howitzers.

Having assembled off Morotai in late June, and after a series of landing exercises there, the Balikpapan Attack Force put to sea on 26 June, under the command of Adm Noble. This assemblage of over 100 American and Australian ships enjoyed decent weather during their 750-mile voyage through the Celebes Sea, but it was still an uncomfortable passage for the men in the cramped landing craft. On 29 June, the bombardment force detached itself and raced ahead of the invasion fleet to begin its final pre-invasion bombardment of the beaches. During the early hours of 1 July, the invasion force reached its position eight miles to the south of the landing beaches. The naval bombardment by six cruisers and 14 destroyers began before dawn, and continued until the first wave of landing craft were approaching

the beach. At the same time, the Japanese defences were attacked by a formation of 63 American Liberator bombers. Everything had been done to support the amphibious assault. From then on it was up to the troops themselves.

The Landing

The plan called for an initial landing by two brigades, with Brig Frederick Chilton's 18th Bde on the left, on Red and Yellow beaches, while Brig Ivan Dougherty's 21st Bde would land on their right, on Green Beach. Shortly after dawn the assault troops moved from their transports – the same ones used in *Oboe 1* – to their smaller landing craft.

Soldiers of the 2/14th Bttn of 21st Bde, disembarking from a US Navy LCI on Green Beach near Balikpapan, on 1 July. Although the landing was unopposed, the battalion was soon in action during its drive northwards from the beachhead up the Vesey Highway.

Australian infantry of the 2/12th Bttn of 18th Bde, crossing the Vesey Highway near Red Beach, after landing near Balikpapan on 1 July. They would then push inland, towards the high ground beyond the beachhead. The smoke behind them probably came from burning oil tanks.

These were a mixture of Alligators, LCVPs and DUKWs, all with American crews. These landing craft moved into their assembly areas off the beaches, while the ferocious naval bombardment continued. In all, over 17,000 shells were fired that morning. At 0850hrs, the bombardment moved further inland; a move timed to coincide with the amphibious landing. At 0900hrs exactly, the 2/10th and 2/12th Bttns of the 18th Bde landed on Red Beach. They encountered no opposition, and quickly established control of the beachhead. On their right, the 2/27th Bttn of 21st Bde landed on Yellow Beach – 800yds to the left of their intended landing place on Green Beach. Again, apart from the odd Japanese shell or mortar round, and some small-arms fire, the landing was completely unopposed.

It took around 15 minutes to fully secure the beach, and then the troops moved inland, the 2/10th heading towards the village of Parramatta to the north and Hill 87 to the north-west. Both positions overlooked the Milford Highway, the road that led northwards towards Balikpapan. The job of the 18th Bde was to secure the high ground to the north of Klandasan, which covered the direct approach to Balikpapan, through Klandasan and over the Parramatta Ridge. The 2/12th headed north too, to the right of the 2/10th, to secure the high ground overlooking the beachhead. By 1030hrs, the 2/12th had advanced some 2,000yds inland, and had passed through Parramatta, and advanced as far as the ridges of high ground at 'Newcastle' and 'Portee' beyond it. Here, though, the Japanese resistance stiffened, and the leading company found itself pinned down.

The 21st Bde, on the right, only had one battalion ashore in the first wave, but its job was two-fold – to secure and expand the bridgehead, and to advance up the coast road to capture the two Japanese airfields to the north-east. So, once ashore, the 2/27th fanned out, with a company advancing east up the coast road (the Vesey Highway), while the rest moved to clear the string of settlements and knolls to the north-east of the beachhead. Just like Tarakan and Labuan, key terrain features were given codenames by the Australian planners. The 2/27th advanced to take the knolls codenamed 'Romilly', 'Ration' and 'Rottnest', all of which were taken without anything more than token resistance from the Japanese. This was largely due to the devastating bombardment, which had forced the bulk of the defenders to withdraw to their defensive positions further inland.

Infantry of 2/10th Bttn of 18th Bde advancing inland towards Balikpapan on 1 July, after securing the beachhead. By nightfall, the battalion had advanced northwards through the village of Parramatta to reach the point inland codenamed 'Newcastle', a mile and a half from Red Beach.

By 1030hrs, however, when the right-hand company of the 2/12th relieved the 2/27th on Ration, they came under increasingly heavy fire from Japanese positions on the higher ground to the north – a pair of knolls, 'Plug' and 'Parkes'. This, it appeared, formed part of the main Japanese defensive line. These Japanese positions were avoided for the moment, as the Australians built up their strength. When a second battalion of the 21st Bde came ashore, the 2/16th, it was quickly sent off to the north-east, and after relieving the 2/27th on Rottnest, it advanced on to secure 'Ravenshoe'. It was a low ridge that led to Mount Malang, further to the east. This was an anchor of the Japanese line, and it had been pounded heavily by both artillery and aircraft. The 2/16th were then ordered to prepare to assault this key Japanese position. It fell shortly before 1700hrs that evening, an hour before nightfall.

Meanwhile, to the east of the bridgehead, the 2/27th Bttn had run into Japanese defences on Charlie's Spur, 1,000yds up the road from Green Beach. The spur was eventually cleared of defenders by 1230hrs, and the battalion's leading companies pressed on to their first main objective, the airfield at Sepinggan. Then the brigade's third battalion, the 2/14th, passed through the 2/27th, and captured the bridge over the Klandasan Besar River. This opened the way towards the fishing village of Stalkudo immediately beyond it, and the coastal road leading off towards the north-east. The brigade consolidated its position, as all spare assets such as tanks, flamethrowers and artillery support were channelled to support the 2/16th and its assault on Mount Malang. It was therefore to the 2/5th Commando Sqn to clear Stalkudo, and then continue east to occupy the high ground beyond it.

During the late afternoon, the bridgehead was strengthened when, on the left, the 2/10th finally cleared the last of the Japanese from Parramatta, while to the north, the leading companies around Newcastle were hit by a string of unexpected Japanese counter-attacks. They held on, and once Parramatta fell, the battalion's front line was strengthened. On the left flank, another freshly landed battalion of the 18th Bde, the 2/9th, headed west towards Klandasan, and captured Santosa Hill, which had blocked the route into the suburb from the beachhead.

AMPHIBIOUS LANDING AT RED BEACH, BALIKPAPAN (PP.80–81)

The largest amphibious operation of the campaign, and the last major one of the entire war, was Operation *Oboe 2*. This was the landing of the Australian 7th Inf Div near Balikpapan on Borneo's eastern coast. This large oil port was a key strategic objective, and so was extremely well defended. Therefore, the port and its defences were extensively bombed in the weeks preceding the landing. Then, on 1 July 1945, a naval task force bombarded the beach defences ahead of the assault, supported by air strikes. The aim was to saturate the defences before the Australian troops stepped ashore. The landing area lay to the east of the port, and was divided into three beaches, Green, Yellow and Red.

This shows the approach of the Australian 2/12th Bttn to Red Beach just before 0900hrs on 1 July. The Australians were transported aboard LCVPs (Landing Craft Vehicle, Personnel) crewed by the US Navy (1). Each carried a platoon of Australian infantry, most of whom were veterans of the North African and New Guinea campaigns (2). To their left, the 2/10th (3) landed a little to the west on the same beach. Many of the LVP-1 Alligators (4) pictured here carried an advanced wave of Australian engineers, charged with clearing any remaining beach defences before the next waves arrived. The shoreline of Red Beach (5) proved largely devoid of defenders after the intense naval bombardment. Behind the beach, the smoke from burning oil tanks outside Balikpapan (6) can be seen, which rose hundreds of feet into the air. In the end, the landing would go smoothly, enabling this leading wave of attackers to press inland, after rapidly securing the beachhead.

As darkness fell, the Australians consolidated their bridgehead and prepared for a resumption of the attack the following morning. Maj Gen Milford was pleasantly surprised that the battle for the bridgehead had gone so well, which extended almost three miles from east to west, and more than a mile to the north. Most of this was due to the prolonged pounding of the Japanese defences by naval bombardment and airstrikes. These then, were proving the key to success in Borneo. Dawn on Monday 2 July came at 0615hrs. That was when the bombardment resumed, augmented this time by the division's artillery, which had come ashore and was deployed close to the Vesey Highway.

Sappers of the 2/9th Field Coy searching for mines during the expansion of the beachhead near Balikpapan on 1 July. During this campaign, the Japanese made extensive use of mines, IEDs and booby traps, and Australian engineers became adept at detecting them.

It was clear that the Japanese had been taken by surprise at the speed of the Australian advance the previous day, as strong defensive positions in the area from Parramatta to Stalkudo had been abandoned as the Japanese withdrew inland, and they still had not been reoccupied before they were overrun by the Australians. The next day, Milford expected that the Japanese would put up more effective resistance. His intention for the Monday was to expand the bridgehead by advancing up the coast to Sepinggan, while securing Klandasan and the axis of the Milford Highway, while also driving the Japanese from the high ground to the west of Mount Malang.

That morning the key battleground was around the point known as 'Potts', to the east of Parramatta, which was still held by a Japanese garrison. It denied the 18th Bde access to the Milford Highway, and so it had to be captured. The 2/12th achieved this during the morning, supported by Matilda tanks and flamethrowers. However, the highway was still overlooked by the Japanese on Hill 87, to the south-west of Parramatta. This high ground was protected by a network of bunkers, tunnels and trenches, and so it was pounded by naval guns and artillery, before the 2/10th began a systematic assault on this vital position. Again, tanks and flamethrowers were used to clear the bunkers, while engineers accompanying the infantry dealt with the network of tunnels using explosives. By nightfall, the hill was largely in Australian hands, although pockets of Japanese troops remained.

By this time, the 25th Bde had come ashore, and at 1430hrs, its 2/31st Bttn was ordered forward up the Milford Highway to clear the Japanese from the knolls known as 'Nurse' and 'Nobody'. This placed the Australians to the east of Balikpapan itself, cutting off the Japanese defenders around Klandasan and the high ground immediately to the south of the port. On the Australian right flank, the 2/14th Bttn advanced steadily up the Vesey Highway, and by 1300hrs, its leading company had taken Sepinggan airfield – a key objective. Meanwhile the bridgehead west of the Klandasan Besar River was cleared of Japanese pockets, and the 21st Bde's position on Mount Malang was reinforced and strengthened. Artillery observers there had a good view over the tree-covered ridges that formed the battleground to the north and west.

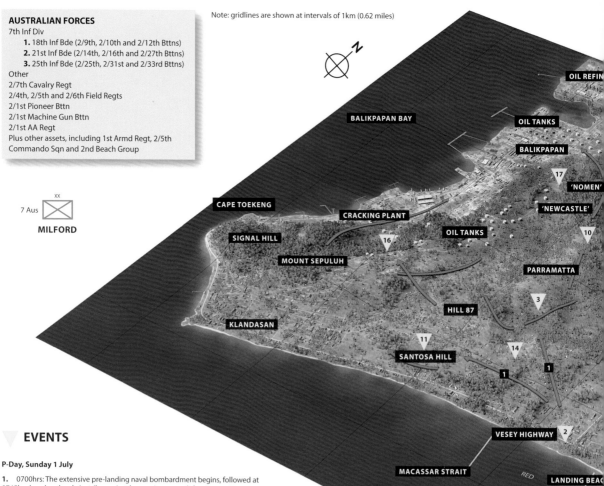

Note: gridlines are shown at intervals of 1km (0.62 miles)

AUSTRALIAN FORCES

7th Inf Div
1. 18th Inf Bde (2/9th, 2/10th and 2/12th Bttns)
2. 21st Inf Bde (2/14th, 2/16th and 2/27th Bttns)
3. 25th Inf Bde (2/25th, 2/31st and 2/33rd Bttns)
Other
2/7th Cavalry Regt
2/4th, 2/5th and 2/6th Field Regts
2/1st Pioneer Bttn
2/1st Machine Gun Bttn
2/1st AA Regt
Plus other assets, including 1st Armd Regt, 2/5th
Commando Sqn and 2nd Beach Group

7 Aus **MILFORD**

OIL REFIN
BALIKPAPAN BAY
OIL TANKS
BALIKPAPAN
'NOMEN' 17
CAPE TOEKENG
CRACKING PLANT 'NEWCASTLE'
SIGNAL HILL 16 OIL TANKS 10
MOUNT SEPULUH
PARRAMATTA
HILL 87 3
KLANDASAN
11 14
SANTOSA HILL 1 1
VESEY HIGHWAY 2
MACASSAR STRAIT RED
LANDING BEAC

▽ EVENTS

P-Day, Sunday 1 July

1. 0700hrs: The extensive pre-landing naval bombardment begins, followed at 0745hrs by a low-level air strike against known Japanese defensive positions, as well as the coast immediately adjacent to the landing beaches. At 0740hrs, the Japanese positions are pounded by a force of 62 US Liberator bombers. The naval bombardment of the coast continues until 0850hrs, when it moves inland.

2. 0900hrs: The 18th Bde's 2/10th and 2/12th Bttns land on Red Beach, encountering no opposition. Simultaneously, the 21st Bde's 2/27th Bttn lands on Yellow Beach.

3. 0915hrs: After securing the beachhead, the 2/10th advance on Parramatta, and Hill 87. By 1210hrs, the hill is secured, despite Japanese resistance, and the village is taken after a set-piece attack at 1412hrs.

4. 1010hrs: The 2/27th presses inland to capture points 'Romilly', 'Ration' and 'Rottnest'. Only light opposition is encountered.

5. 1020hrs: 'Portee' and 'Newcastle' are captured by a company of the 2/12th but are counter-attacked. They dig in and hold their positions around Portee until dawn, fighting off four more attacks.

6. 1030hrs: The 2/12th occupies Ration but is drawn into a fight with Japanese defenders on 'Parkes' and 'Plug'. These positions were taken by 1700hrs, with the help of the 2/27th Bttn, supported by tanks, artillery bombardments and flamethrowers.

7. 1100hrs: The 2/16th Bttn of 21st Bde lands on Green Beach and moves through the 2/27th to occupy 'Ravenshoe'. It then advances on Mount Malang, which is secured by 1650hrs after a protracted firefight.

8. 1115hrs: A Coy of the 2/27th comes under heavy fire from Charlie's Spur. It is cleared of the enemy by 1230hrs.

9. 1500hrs: After landing in the second wave, the 2/14th Bttn reaches Charlie's Spur and presses on to capture the bridge Klandasan Besar bridge without opposition. At 1630hrs, the 2/5th Commando Sqn passes through it to clear Stalkudo village, and the high ground beyond it.

10. 1515hrs: After securing Parramatta, the 2/10th send patrols forward to occupy Newcastle.

11. 1815hrs: As dusk descends, the 2/9th Bttn captures Santosa Hill, on the eastern outskirts of Klandasan.

P-Day +1, Monday 2 July

12. 0915hrs: The 2/14th advances north up the Vesey Highway, to capture the Japanese airfield at Sepinggan. It is captured by 1300hrs.

13. 1000hrs: The 2/27th strengthens its hold on Mount Malang and links up with the 2/3rd Commando Sqn on the far side of the Klandasan Besar River.

14. 1025hrs: the 2/12th clears 'Potts' of the enemy, while the 2/10th systematically clears the area around Parramatta and Hill 87, using explosives to destroy bunkers and tunnels. This takes most of the day.

15. 1420hrs: The 2/31st of the reserve 25th Bde advances up the Milford Highway to secure 'Nurse' and 'Nobody'.

16. 1520hrs: Mount Sepuluh is captured by the 2/10th, which also captures the cracking plant there after a tough fight. The Australians now overlook Balikpapan port.

P-Day +2, Tuesday 3 July

17. 1100hrs: The 2/10th advances through Parramatta and 'Nomen' to enter Balikpapan. The heavily damaged port is captured, although pockets of Japanese resistance remain. Other pockets in Klandasan are also mopped up.

18. 1300hrs: The 2/31st secures the crossing over the Sumber River, while to its right the 2/33rd, also of the 25th Bde, clear the area around Dougherty's Road.

Although mopping-up operations continue for another two days, the bridgehead is now secure, supplies are being brought ashore and work begins on clearing Balikpapan port. The Australian 7th Div can now begin extending its hold of eastern Borneo.

THE BATTLE FOR BALIKPAPAN, 1–3 JULY 1945

The attack on the oil port of Balikpapan in eastern Borneo was the last major amphibious operation of the war. It involved landing the veteran Australian 7th Inf Div in its entirety, supported by additional armour. Facing them was the largest Japanese garrison force in Borneo, whose formidable defences included coastal batteries, pillboxes, tunnels and well-constructed defensive lines. The landing on 1 July was largely unopposed, however, due to an extensive bombardment from warships and aircraft. The Australians quickly fanned out to secure the beachhead, and the steep hills which overlooked it. On the left, the 18th Inf Bde fought its way into Klandasan, before advancing on Balikpapan from the east, while the 21st Inf Bde concentrated on securing the coast road, which led north to two Japanese airfields. The port was finally captured on 3 July, but mopping-up operations lasted for two more days.

DANSARI

SUMBER RIVER

18

'NAIL'

GRAHA INDA

DOUGHERTY'S ROAD

ERVOIR 'NURSE' 15 'NOBODY'

MILFORD HIGHWAY

'OXYGEN'

'PORTEE'

3

'OXLEY' 'ORANGE'

OTTS'

'OWEN' MOUNT MALANG

'PARKES'

KLANDASAN BESAR RIVER

1

LUG' 13

6

'RATION' 7

'RECORD'

4 'RAVENSHOE'

'ROTTNEST'

2

'ROMILLY' 8

2 CHARLIE'S SPUR

9 STALKUDO 12

GREEN

22 SBF ⚓ ˣ

KAMADA

JAPANESE FORCES
Balikpapan Garrison
22nd Naval Special Base Force
71st Independent Mixed Bde
432nd, 454th, 455th, 553rd and 554th Bttns
774th Independent Bttn

At 1400hrs, as the 2/10th Bttn was mopping up on Hill 87, two companies were sent forward to climb the eastern slopes of Mount Sepuluh, the heights which separated Balikpapan and Klandasan. The Australians reached the summit, but the firefight around the cracking plant and oil tanks there continued well into the evening. As on Hill 87, their opponents were troops from the 454th Independent Inf Bttn and the 2nd Garrison Force. The heavily battered cracking plant was eventually captured by the 2/10th that evening. With it in Australian hands, Balikpapan was within reach of the Australians. Sure enough, the Japanese seemed to agree, as despite Japanese company-level counter-attacks during the night on Mount Sepuluh and the 2/12th positions around Newcastle and Nomen, the night passed relatively peaceably.

The reason became clear at dawn. The bulk of the Japanese garrison had withdrawn from Balikpapan during the night, and had moved six miles further to the north-east, around the village of Batuchampar, on the Milford Highway. So, on the morning of Tuesday 3 July, the 2/10th descended the ridge near Nomen, and the 2/9th advanced through Pandansari, both without encountering more than scattered groups of Japanese troops. By 1100hrs, these leading elements of the 18th Bde had entered the port. However, the Australians would spend much of the rest of the day dealing with isolated pockets of Japanese resistance. The same happened in Klandasan, which was cleared throughout the day by two companies of the 2/9th. Both the port and the suburb had been extensively mined and booby-trapped, and it would take the division's engineers several days to clear them.

Meanwhile, that Tuesday morning, the Australian 25th Bde, which was leading the pursuit, advanced up the Milford Highway to cut off the route from Batuchampar and Balikpapan. While the brigade's 2/31st Bttn reached the Sumber River and secured Orr's Crossing, which safeguarded the eastern side of the oil refinery complex at Pandansari to the north of Balikpapan, the 2/33rd pressed on up the highway to clear the area around Batuchampar and the dirt track leading east from it known as Dougherty's Road. Effectively, although mopping-up operations would continue, the bridgehead was now secure. Supplies were brought ashore in increasing numbers, so the division could rest, replenish and prepare for whatever challenges lay ahead.

After Australian troops entered Balikpapan on 3 July, they had to clear the port of any remaining pockets of Japanese troops. Here, men of the 2/10th Bttn clear the oil refinery on the northern side of the port, supported by a troop of Matilda tanks. The fire is from oil facilities set ablaze by the Japanese as they withdrew.

In fact, what followed was something of an anti-climax. On 5 July, two battalions and a commando detachment were landed at Penajam on the west side of Balikpapan Bay to capture the Japanese coastal artillery batteries. This enabled the Allies to bring supplies into the port, once it had been cleared of mines and booby traps, and damaged infrastructure repaired. In the meantime, American engineers had built landing stages and piers on the landing beaches. Fighting continued around Batuchampar, which delayed the Australian expansion of their perimeter until 21 July. This, however, was little more than a rear-guard action, and over the next few days it gave ground in the

Once ashore near Balikpapan, the 21st Bde advanced to secure the airfields at Sepinggan and Manggar. This sketch from the war diary of the 2/14th Bttn shows Japanese positions on the high ground overlooking Manggar airfield.

face of concerted attacks by the 25th Bde, supported by tanks and artillery. Eventually, the heavily depleted Japanese rear guard withdrew into the interior of Borneo, in the general area of the Sambodja oilfields.

Patrols were then sent out to various points along the coast to east and west, transported by landing craft, while Australian spearheads continued to press up the Milford Highway. The airfield of Manggar was also captured on 21 July. At that point, Maj Gen Milford called a halt to any further large-scale offensive operations, although minor clashes between patrols would continue until the armistice some three weeks later. In late August, despite the ceasefire, elements of the 22nd Naval Special Base Force tried to infiltrate Balikpapan by boat from the western side of the bay. This, however, was thwarted after a few small skirmishes.

Oboe 2, the capture of Balikpapan, was the final major operation of the Borneo campaign, and arguably the last one of the entire Pacific War, apart from the Soviet invasion of Manchuria. It cost the lives of 229 Australian soldiers, while another 622 were wounded. Japanese casualties were placed at 2,032 killed and 63 captured, although the real number might have been higher as many more Japanese troops were missing at the end of the war. The value of the whole operation has been questioned, but it undoubtedly gained political and military prestige for Australia on the eve of negotiations that would establish the future course of the entire Pacific basin.

Whatever its strategic benefits were, there is no doubt that *Oboe 2* was extremely well organized and implemented. A key part in this success was the naval and logistical support offered to the Australian I Corps by the United States, particularly in the supply of a task force, landing ships, air support and vast mountains of supplies. This enabled Maj Gen Milford to expend large quantities of munitions, reducing casualties during the closing weeks of the war. Without American help, the number of Australian lives lost would undoubtedly have been considerably higher.

The small and precarious airfield control tower at Manggar airfield to the north of Balikpapan was used by a naval observation team during the battle for control of the airfield on 4–9 July. Although the Australian 2/14th Bttn captured the airfield, the Japanese held the jungle-clad high ground overlooking it to the north, and naval gunfire played a crucial part in driving them off.

AFTERMATH

In the few weeks from 1 May to 15 August, the Australian I Corps had secured the islands of Tarakan and Labuan, gained control of most of British Borneo and established themselves ashore in a secure beachhead at Balikpapan in Dutch Borneo. The cost of all this had been high. The Australians suffered around 2,100 casualties – killed, wounded or missing. It was a high price for what was essentially an unnecessary campaign, fought during the closing months of the war. This, though, is a viewpoint which benefits from hindsight. Despite rumours, neither the Australian government nor its army were aware that the dropping of two atomic bombs in early August would lead to a cessation of hostilities.

After all, plans had already been developed for follow-up operations in the Celebes and on Java. The invasion of Borneo formed part of MacArthur's broad strategy, highlighted in Operation *Montclair*, which was primarily aimed at wresting the Dutch East Indies from the Japanese. Operation *Oboe* was merely part of that grand design – one which was cut short by the ceasefire. Seen in this light, the invasion of Borneo was a valid operation, with a viable strategic purpose. It was the sudden onset of peace that rendered it an unnecessary and costly venture. This said, there was little enthusiasm in Washington for wasting men and resources on what was essentially a potentially costly mopping-up operation in the East Indies, waged in a region which had already been bypassed.

Soldiers from C Coy, 2/24th Bttn pictured on Tarakan after the battle, displaying trophies of war. In the front row (left) is the company commander, Capt Eldridge. After the battle, the 26th Bde remained on Tarakan until the end of the war.

In Borneo, the announcement of a ceasefire had come after the major fighting had ceased. However, patrolling continued, and minor clashes still occurred in North Borneo and to the north of Balikpapan in Dutch Borneo. By then though, the Australian senior commanders and politicians had already moved their focus from Borneo to other pastures – either Java or Sumatra or the Japanese homeland. At the time, plans had been drawn up to create a British Commonwealth Corps, which would include an Australian infantry division, as well as British, Indian and New Zealand ones, to operate alongside the Americans in Operation *Olympus* – the

The after-effects of the naval bombardment of the Brunei coast near Brooketon during the landings there on 10 June. Here, three RAAF personnel inspect the damage to the palm-fringed beach east of the town. In fact, the landing on Green Beach there was completely unopposed.

invasion of Japan itself. Planning for this was quickly overtaken by the events which followed the dropping of the two atom bombs.

Early on 10 August, after intense debate and internal rebellion, the Japanese government advised Emperor Hirohito that Japan had no real option but to surrender. While it took time to convince the emperor, and to agree terms with the Allies, the decision to surrender was finally made on 14 August. The following day, at noon in Tokyo, a recorded radio address by Emperor Hirohito was broadcast, announcing Japan's capitulation. To avoid confusion, this was followed on 17 August by orders for all Japanese military forces to immediately lay down their arms.

This prompted immediate VJ Day celebrations across the globe, although in the United States, official observation was reserved for the final act of surrender on 2 September. Generally, despite the ceasefire beginning at noon on 15 August, it took time for word of the end of hostilities to reach all the Japanese in Borneo. To help things along, the Australians established radio communications with the Japanese army commanders in the theatre, ceasefire announcements were transmitted by radio and leaflets were dropped over the jungle in areas where Japanese troops were likely to be. Once links with the 37th Army command had been established, Lt Gen Morshead organized the dropping of supplies for Allied POWs near Sandakan and Kuching.

In most cases though, Japanese commanders waited for official orders to be passed down to them from their superiors. However, on 3 September, Lt Gen Baba commanding the 37th Army was transported to Labuan, where he officially surrendered his forces to Maj Gen Wootten of the 9th Inf Div. Five days later, on 8 September, V Adm Kamada did the same to Maj Gen Milford of the 7th Inf Div. This capitulation took place aboard the frigate HMAS *Burdekin* lying off the Mahakam River, 75 miles north of Balikpapan.

Japanese POWs disembark from a barge on the Padas River, after surrendering to Australians of the 24th Bde in North Borneo, on 18 August, in the immediate aftermath of the ceasefire. They were held in a prisoner of war compound near Beaufort, before being transported to a more secure facility at Jesselton.

The following day Lt Gen Teshima of the 2nd Army did the same in Morotai. This effectively ended organized Japanese resistance across much of the East Indies.

Borneo was then divided up, with British Borneo administered by Wootten's division, and Dutch Borneo by Milford's command. Each of these areas was divided into military zones, where elements of these two divisions would supervise the surrender of Japanese troops, the collection of weapons and the distribution of food and medical supplies. On 11 September, Allied troops landed at Kuching, to secure the surrender of the Japanese forces there commanded by Maj Gen Yamamura. It also led to the liberation of Allied prisoners of war. Hundreds of these, many of them from the Indian army, were flown to Labuan for medical treatment, recovery and then repatriation.

Some Japanese groups, however, refused to surrender. The largest band of these was in northern Sarawak. For the most part, Wootten left it to Sarawak guerrillas and Dyak tribesmen to harry them, and 346 of them surrendered on 29 October. By the end of the month, the Allies calculated that in British Borneo some 17,000 Japanese troops and 4,000 Japanese civilians were held as prisoners of war, the majority in Kuching or Jesselton in North Borneo. In Dutch Borneo, another 6,600 prisoners were held at Samarinda, north of Balikpapan. This effectively brought an end to hostilities, save for the last scattered remnants still at large. The Australians could then devote their efforts to supporting the civilian population, restoring civil government and repatriating Allied POWs.

By then though, the Australians had learned of the grim fate of most of the Allied prisoners of war who had been incarcerated in Borneo. The POW camp at Sandakan in North Borneo had held thousands of Allied prisoners, many of whom had been captured when Singapore fell in early 1942. Conditions in the camp had been horrendous, and by early 1945, less than 1,900 of these POWs remained alive. At that point, on the orders of Lt Gen Baba, 470 of them were escorted inland to the hill town of Ranau, 160 miles to the south-west. Only a handful survived the journey. This was the first of what became known as the Sandakan Death Marches.

Ironically, Baba had ordered the march in response to the increasing threat of Allied invasion. Two more death marches followed. During the first, in March 1945, 536 malnourished prisoners were sent to Ranau, of whom 353 died on the way. That left around 250 prisoners at Sandakan, who were essentially left to starve to death. However, in June, 75 of the fittest were led away towards Ranau. None of them lived to complete the journey. Those starving prisoners remaining in Sandakan all died before the ceasefire. The remaining 38 prisoners at Ranau were then shot by their guards, several days after the end of hostilities. Six Australian servicemen managed to escape during the marches and survived to give evidence. As a result, Lt Gen Baba was executed for war crimes, as were several camp commanders. Afterwards, it was felt that more could have been done by the Allies to save the POWs, and the controversy continued long after Japan's final surrender.

Similarly, the debate about the value of the Borneo campaign would continue after the war. Certainly, mistakes were made. For instance, Tarakan, the costliest of the Australian operations, was largely unnecessary as an airfield was available at Tawi-Tawi in the Sulu Archipelago. It was clear that in British Borneo and at Balikpapan, the Japanese withdrew into the island's interior when faced with overwhelming force. At Tarakan, and again at Labuan, there was nowhere else for the Japanese to go. So, they stood their ground and fought to the death. This said, it was clear that the amphibious operations and the land battle that followed were conducted effectively by an Australian army that was at the top of its professional game. In this respect, the Borneo campaign can be seen as a high point of Australian arms during World War II, a culmination of a military record that led from North Africa and New Guinea to the shores of Borneo.

Dyak irregulars in Brunei, June 1945. During the years of Japanese occupation, Borneo's indigenous Dyaks fought a low-level guerrilla war against the occupants. After the Allied invasion, they cooperated with the Australians in hunting down pockets of Japanese resistance in the island's hinterland.

A stretcher party carrying a wounded man back to the casualty clearing station on Red Beach, Balikpapan, on 1 July. These were established within an hour of the beachhead being secured, and serious casualties were quickly transported to sick bays aboard the larger transport ships.

THE BATTLEFIELD TODAY

Much of the terrain fought over by Australian and Japanese troops during Operation *Oboe* has changed beyond recognition. Borneo underwent extensive political and economic change in the aftermath of the war. In August 1945, a proclamation of independence by the Indonesians brought about a four-year war of independence. By its end, the Dutch ceded control of their East Indies colonies, and the country of Indonesia was created, with its capital in Jakarta. Dutch Borneo became the Indonesian province of Kalimantan, which underwent an economic revival. As a result, the two *Oboe* battlegrounds of Tarakan and Balikpapan have become heavily built over. While a similar post-war expansion also took place in Sarawak, Brunei and North Borneo (now known as Sabah), this had less of an impact on the island's battlefields.

On Tarakan, the town of 1945 has become a sprawling city of a quarter of a million inhabitants. The wartime airfield is now the site of Juwata International Airport, but surprisingly, this was built on the footprint of the original Japanese field. A visitor there can still determine the basic layout. The landing beaches have been built over, becoming part of the city's port. Still, it is not impossible to trace the location of the beaches, largely because the old wartime road network has remained unchanged. Tank Hill remains, a legacy of the now largely redundant oil facilities of the island.

Tarakan City has encompassed the villages and outlying districts of the old town. Residential areas cover the ground fought over in the days following the landing. However, further inland the terrain remains much as it was. It is still possible to explore the sites of the bitter fighting for Fukukaku, and wartime traces can still be found in the shape of the remains of Japanese defences. Parts of this area, however, are in private or corporate ownership, and access is limited.

The other island that was fought over, Labuan, has also changed, because of urban expansion. The landing beaches are still there, and Victoria itself is largely unchanged. Further inland, Flagstaff Hill and the Pocket have been built over, and little remains of their wartime appearance. However, one can still trace the extent of both features, while much of the mangrove swamp to the east of the Pocket remains. The island's main wartime airfield is now Labuan Airport, but like Tarakan, the layout there remains unchanged.

Some 16 miles to the south-west, the landing beaches near Brunei remain largely unaltered, although Yellow Beach is now part of the Muara Port complex, and Muara Island now boasts a pair of chemical plants. Today, the road from the beaches to Brunei town runs through suburbs rather than forest, but the hamlets fought over near the wartime airfield are still identifiable. The airfield is now Brunei International Airport, while Brunei itself is now Bandar Seri Begawan, an affluent and expansive city, dominated by its mosque complex and Sultan's palace.

Elsewhere, the areas of Brunei and Sarawak that were fought over during the campaign are largely unchanged. This is also true of North Borneo. Here the landing beaches of Weston and Mempakul are much as they were, as are the banks of the Padas and Klias. The route from Weston to Beaufort has also hardly altered. In Beaufort itself, which has expanded considerably, it is still possible to trace the course of the battle, as the high ground around the town remains largely undeveloped. This is particularly true on the town's eastern side, where a visitor can readily understand how the high ground there overlooked the Japanese line of retreat.

Finally, the battlefield of Balikpapan has altered significantly because of urban expansion. Still, the landing beaches themselves are largely unchanged, although immediately behind them the coastal road (the wartime Vesey Highway) now runs through residential areas. Further inland, a golf course covers the ground fought over during the expansion of the beachhead to the north-east, while to the north-west, the area around Parramatta is covered by housing. This makes it extremely difficult to identify the key features of the battlefield. Nevertheless, the ridge dividing Klandasan and Balikpapan is a useful orientation point, and a trip up it is rewarded with a view of the landing beaches on one side and the port on the other.

While disappointing for the battlefield visitor, with patience, the basic salient features of the *Oboe 2* battleground can still be traced. For instance, the layout of the wartime Sepinggan airfield, which was expanded into the Sultan Aji Muhammad Sulaiman Sepinggan International Airport can be identified, as can the small village of Stalkudo. Further to the north, in the direction of Batuchampar, the landscape is largely unchanged and gives a good impression of what the whole area would have looked like in 1945. So, in brief, the battlefields of Borneo 1945 are still there if a visitor is prepared to look for them. Then, armed with wartime maps and photographs, it is still possible – with a little imagination – to trace the course of the fighting.

The Labuan War Cemetery was established close to the scene of the heavy fighting for the island in May 1945, two miles north of the town of Victoria and close to the main Japanese airfield, now the site of the island's main airport. Almost 3,000 Allied troops are interred there, the majority of whom died in the 'death camps' near Sandakan and Kuching.

FURTHER READING

Bell, Roger, *Unequal Allies: Australian–American Relations and the Pacific War*, Melbourne University Press: Melbourne, Australia (1997)

Converse, Allan, *Armies of Empire: The 9th Australian and 50th British Divisions in Battle 1939–45*, Cambridge University Press: Cambridge (2011)

Costello, John, *The Pacific War 1941–45*, Harper Perennial: New York, USA (2006 reprint)

Coulthard-Clark, Chris, *The Encyclopaedia of Australia's Battles*, Allen & Unwin: St Leonards, New South Wales, Australia (2001)

Coulthard-Clark, Chris, *Where Australians Fought: The Encyclopaedia of Australia's Battles*, Allen & Unwin: St Leonards, New South Wales, Australia (2008)

Dean, Peter J. (ed.), *Australia, 1944–45: Victory in the Pacific*, Cambridge University Press: Melbourne, Australia (2016)

Dean, Peter J. *MacArthur's Coalition: US and Australian Operations in the Southwest Pacific Area, 1942–45*, University Press of Kansas: Lawrence, Kansas, USA (2018)

Dennis, Peter, *The Oxford Companion to Australian Military History*, Oxford University Press: Melbourne, Australia (1996)

Fitzpatrick, Georgina, McCormack, L. H. and Morris, Narrelle (eds), *Australia's War Crime Trials, 1945–51*, Brill Nijhoff: Leiden, The Netherlands (2016)

Galloway, Jack, *The Odd Couple: Blamey and MacArthur at War*, Brisbane University Press: Brisbane, Australia (2006)

Grey, Geoffrey, *The Australian Army: A History*, Cambridge University Press: Melbourne, Australia (2006)

Hastings, Max, *Nemesis: The Battle for Japan, 1944–45*, Harper Press: London (2007)

Horner, David, *Blamey: the Commander-in-Chief*, Allen & Unwin: Sydney, Australia (1998)

Keogh, Eustace, *The South West Pacific 1941–45*, Grayflower Productions: Melbourne, Australia (1965)

Long, Gavin, *Australia in the War of 1939–45: The Final Campaigns*, Australian War Memorial: Canberra, Australia (1963)

Long, Gavin, *Australia in the War of 1939–45: The Six Years War*, Australian War Memorial: Canberra, Australia (1973)

MacArthur, Douglas (ed.), *The Campaigns of MacArthur in the Pacific*, US Army Center of Military History: Washington, DC, USA (1946)

McKenzie-Smith, Graham, *The Unit Guide: The Australian Army, 1939–45*, Big Sky Publishing: Warriewood, New South Wales, Australia (2018)

Ministry of Defence, *War with Japan: The Advance on Japan*, HMSO: London (1995)

Odgers, George, *Australia in the War of 1939–45: Air War Against Japan, 1943–45*, Australian War Memorial: Canberra, Australia (1957)

Ooi, Keat Jin, *The Japanese Occupation of Borneo, 1941–45*, Routledge: London (2010)

Stanley, Peter, *Tarakan: An Australian Tragedy*, Allen & Unwin: Sydney, Australia (1997)

Thompson, Peter, *Pacific Fury: How Australia and her Allies Defeated the Japanese Scourge*, William Heinemann: Sydney, Australia (2008)

INDEX

Figures in **bold** refer to illustrations.